MILAN TRAVEL GUIDE 2023

The Complete Guide to Discover Milan and The Italian Lakes | A Tapestry of History, Food, Culture and Natural Beauty

Jimmy Vitale

MILAN TRAVEL GUIDE 2023

MILAN TRAVEL GUIDE 2023

© Copyright 2023 by Jimmy Vitale - All rights reserved.

All rights reserved. No part of this book may be reproduced in any form without permission in writing from the author. Reviewers may quote brief passages in reviews.

While all attempts have been made to verify the information provided in this publication, neither the author nor the publisher assumes any responsibility for errors, omissions, or contrary interpretation of the subject matter herein.

The views expressed in this publication are those of the author alone and should not be taken as expert instruction or commands. The reader is responsible for his or her own actions, as well as his or her own interpretation of the material found within this publication.

Adherence to all applicable laws and regulations, including international, federal, state and local governing professional licensing, business practices, advertising, and all other aspects of doing business in the US, Canada or any other jurisdiction is the sole responsibility of the reader and consumer.

Neither the author nor the publisher assumes any responsibility or liability whatsoever on behalf of the consumer or reader of this material. Any perceived slight of any individual or organization is purely unintentional.

MILAN TRAVEL GUIDE 2023

Table of Contents

INTRODUCTION 6
   Brief Overview of Milan's Significance as A Cultural and Fashion Hub 7
   Introduction To the Enchanting Italian Lakes Region 8
   Overview Of the Guide's Structure and Purpose 10

BOOK 1 // The City Of Milan 12

Historical Background and Significance 13

Exploring The Iconic Landmarks 17
   Milan Cathedral (Duomo di Milano) 18
   Sforza Castle (Castello Sforzesco) 21
   La Scala Opera House (Teatro alla Scala) 24
   Leonardo da Vinci's Last Supper (Il Cenacolo) 27
   Church of San Maurizio al Monastero Maggiore 29
   Galleria Vittorio Emanuele II 32

Art And Culture in Milan 35
   Brera Art Gallery (Pinacoteca di Brera) 35
   Museum of the Twentieth Century (Museo del Novecento) 38

Design And Fashion Districts 43
   Quadrilatero della Moda 43
   Brera Design District 46

Milanese Cuisine and Local Delicacies 50
   Traditional Dishes and Where to Find Them 50
   Best Restaurants & Street Food Experiences 54

Insider Tips from Locals 58
   Hidden Gems and Lesser-Known Local Attractions 58
   Recommended Local Neighborhoods for Exploration 63

BOOK 2 // The Italian Lakes 66

Introduction to the Italian Lakes Region 67
   Overview of Lake Como, Lake Garda, Lake Maggiore, and Lake Orta 67

Geographical Highlights and Natural Beauty 71

Lake Como **75**

Towns and Attractions in Lake Como 76

Water Sports, Boat Tours, and Hiking Opportunities 79

Lake Garda **83**

Towns and Attractions in Lake Garda 84

Wine Tasting and Outdoor Activities 87

Lake Maggiore **91**

Towns and Attractions in Lake Maggiore 92

Gardens, Palaces, and Scenic Cable Car Rides 94

Lake Orta **98**

Towns and Attractions in Lake Orta 99

Tranquility, Spiritual Retreats, and Local Legends 102

Insider Tips for the Italian Lakes **106**

Best Viewpoints and Scenic Spots 106

Local Festivals and Events 107

Recommendations For Hiking, Boating, And Cycling 108

Smart Tips for Budget Travelers **112**

Affordable Accommodation Options 112

Budget-Friendly Dining and Transportation 113

CONCLUSION **116**

Final Tips and Recommendations for A Perfect Trip 117

Encouragement To Explore Other Regions of Italy 118

Closing Thoughts on The Tapestry of History, Culture, And Natural Beauty 120

MILAN TRAVEL GUIDE 2023

INTRODUCTION

As Italy's second-largest city, **Milan** is an international metropolis with a chic disposition. Soon, you'll find yourself strolling down elegant streets, admiring iconic landmarks like the Gothic-style Duomo di Milano, or immersing yourself in the world of high-fashion at the upscale boutiques of Quadrilatero della Moda. But there's more to this city than just sophistication – its rich history and vibrant contemporary scene blend seamlessly into a fascinating tapestry.

A trip to Milan would not be complete without savoring its mouth-watering cuisine. From perfectly cooked risotto alla Milanese to succulent osso buco, your taste buds are in for a treat as you discover why Italian food is revered worldwide.

Your journey continues beyond the bustling metropolis to the picturesque **Italian Lakes**. This enchanting region is known for its fairytale-like landscapes dotted with colorful towns nestled between imposing mountains and serene waters. Whether you decide to explore romantic Lake Como or adventurous Lake Garda, these bodies of water truly live up to their reputation as some of Italy's most exquisite gems.

Outdoor enthusiasts will revel in the myriad activities available around the lakes. Hiking trails with breathtaking panoramas await intrepid explorers while leisurely boat rides reveal charming lakeside villages perfect for captivating photo opportunities.

Allow this Milan Travel Guide 2023 to be your trusted companion as you unlock all that this exceptional destination has to offer. From uncovering hidden gems in fashionable Milan to basking in the beauty of the Italian Lakes, say "Ciao!" to an unforgettable adventure full of unforgettable memories!

Brief Overview of Milan's Significance as A Cultural and Fashion Hub

Milan, Italy's second-largest city, has established itself as a global icon of culture and fashion. Known worldwide as a hub for high-end design and artwork, Milan is revered in contemporary haute couture. Many Italian designers such as Armani, Versace, and Dolce & Gabbana have found their fortunes within this marvelous metropolitan center.

This vibrant city brims with innovation and centuries-old history. Home to some of the world's greatest icons of art, including Leonardo da Vinci's Last Supper and the glistening golden statue of Madonnina atop the cathedral – there is no shortage of cultural riches to be admired in Milan. The city actively fosters creativity through many museums, galleries, and collections that showcase both historical and modern art.

Aside from its high-end fashion scene, Milan also boasts exceptional architecture. The Cathedral of Milan (Duomo di Milano), a prime example of Gothic architecture, exemplifies the city's rich architectural heritage. Furthermore, Castello Sforzesco reveals military power while Galleria Vittorio Emanuele II highlights elegant shopping experiences.

Music lovers will also find themselves immersed in one of Italy's liveliest cities. La Scala opera house is renowned worldwide for its outstanding performances and historic elegance, while San Siro stadium hosts exciting soccer games that enthrall fans on a regular basis.

Each year, countless visitors flock to this dazzling destination to get a taste of its unparalleled cultural offerings. Milan truly embraces its diverse influences and identities while remaining rooted in a rich history. As you delve into the Milan Travel Guide 2023, prepare yourself for an unforgettable journey through this illustrious city that exudes fashion and art at every turn.

Introduction To the Enchanting Italian Lakes Region

Nestled among the mesmerizing Alpine landscapes of Northern Italy, the Italian Lakes region is a captivating destination that entices travelers with its captivating beauty and timeless charm. The area consists predominantly of four major lakes - Lake Como, Lake Garda, Lake Maggiore, and Lake Orta - each offering its unique allure to visitors from around the world.

The Italian Lakes region is characterized by crystal-clear waters, stunning natural scenery, and picturesque villages dotting the shores. As you journey through this magical region, you cannot help but be enchanted by the azure waters framed by lush hillsides adorned with Mediterranean vegetation and age-old villas steeped in history.

For centuries, poets, artists, and luminaries have been drawn to this idyllic setting seeking inspiration and respite from their everyday lives. Today, you too can experience that same sense of wonder as you stroll through quaint cobblestone streets, indulge in Italian gastronomy at family-owned trattorias or explore scenic walking trails through verdant woods.

Moreover, numerous outdoor activities await your discovery in this beguiling region. From water sports like sailing and windsurfing to hiking and biking through the surrounding hills, there is no shortage of adventures to be had in this captivating haven.

The Italian Lakes region is a place where nature's splendor coexists harmoniously with charming towns imbued with alluring tradition and history. Whether for relaxation or exploration, a visit to this enchanting destination promises an unforgettable experience that will linger in your memory for years to come.

MILAN TRAVEL GUIDE 2023

Overview Of the Guide's Structure and Purpose

"Milan Travel Guide 2023" is a comprehensive guide that offers an in-depth exploration of Milan's rich history, culture, art, and cuisine, as well as the enchanting beauty of the Italian Lakes. Divided into two main sections, the guide caters to various interests and travel preferences, while providing insider tips from locals and smart budget advice.

The first section focuses on Milan and includes historical background information, iconic landmark exploration such as the Milan Cathedral, Sforza Castle, La Scala Opera House, and Leonardo da Vinci's Last Supper. It also delves into the city's vibrant art and culture scene covering galleries like Pinacoteca di Brera and Museo del Novecento. Readers are introduced to design and fashion districts such as Quadrilatero della Moda, Brera Design District, and Porta Nuova District. Culinary indulgence in traditional dishes and local delicacies along with hidden gems enriches the overall Milan experience.

The second section covers the fascinating Italian Lakes region, offering overviews of Lake Como, Lake Garda, Lake Maggiore, and Lake Orta. Detailed information is provided on each lake's towns and attractions such as Bellagio in Lake Como or Sirmione in Lake Garda. Various outdoor activities like water sports, boat tours, wine tasting, hiking

MILAN TRAVEL GUIDE 2023

opportunities are also highlighted. Insider tips for best viewpoints and scenic spots complement suggestions for local festivals, events as well as recommendations for hiking, boating, and cycling activities.

Overall, this guide serves as an invaluable tool for travelers eager to experience the splendors of Milan and the Italian Lakes by providing informative background details along with practical insights from locals to ensure a remarkable journey.

MILAN TRAVEL GUIDE 2023

BOOK 1 // The City Of Milan

MILAN TRAVEL GUIDE 2023

Historical Background and Significance

Milan has long been a city of considerable significance, both culturally and economically, in Italy. Founded around 600 BCE by the Celts and later conquered in 222 BCE by the Romans, Milan played an important role in the Roman Empire. However, the city's deep historical roots encompass various periods - medieval, Renaissance, Napoleonic era, Industrial Revolution, and modern times – all of which continue to contribute to its development as a thriving metropolis.

During the Celtic period, Milan was known as Mediolanum, meaning "middle of the plain", referring to its strategic location in northern Italy. The Romans recognized its potential and conquered it during the Roman-Italic wars. They incorporated Milan into the core of their expanding empire and leveraged its central position by connecting it to other territories through efficient road networks such as Via Aemilia Scauri.

In 313 CE, Emperor Constantine signed the Edict of Milan, a landmark decree legalizing Christianity throughout the Roman Empire. This event ushered in a new era for Milan, making it a pioneer in religious freedom and establishing it as an important center for Christian worship. The early Christian basilicas of

MILAN TRAVEL GUIDE 2023

San Lorenzo Maggiore, Sant'Ambrogio, and San Nazaro Maggiore all bear witness to this period of transformation.

However, it is during the medieval period that Milan's influence truly began to flourish. The powerful House of Visconti ruled for almost two centuries from 1277-1447 CE. Their ambitious aspirations included promoting culture and arts throughout their dominion; one famous example being the construction of Castello Sforzesco in 1358 CE. Through dynastic marriages with other influential families across Europe, they extended their political prowess and established ties with foreign elites.

Their reign ended with Filippo Maria Visconti's death without heirs in 1447; however, their accomplishments created a solid foundation for the emergence of the Sforza dynasty. Under this new ruling family's leadership, Milan thrived in trade and prosperity. It became one of the leading centers of Renaissance art under the patronage of Ludovico il Moro. He commissioned works by Bramante, including the design for Santa Maria delle Grazie, housing Leonardo da Vinci's masterpiece – The Last Supper.

Milan fell temporarily under French rule following Ludovico's death in 1499 CE but was later returned to the Habsburgs during the Italian Wars. With Spanish domination in 1535 CE, Milan suffered a significant economic downturn; however, several cultural institutions were established during this period. In particular, Stampa and Borromeo families founded the Ambrosian Library - Milano's oldest library – and hosted esteemed intellectuals.

The Napoleonic era in the early 19th century brought momentous change to Milan. As part of his expansive kingdom, Napoleon Bonaparte initiated fundamental reforms that laid the groundwork for modern Italian administration and legal systems. The Brera Academy and Museum accrued a vast collection of art, while Galleria Vittorio Emanuele II emerged as a prominent shopping hub and architectural marvel.

Throughout industrial revolution and unification of Italy in the mid-1800s, Milan continued to develop both industrially and strategically. Hosting numerous factories such as Pirelli tires and Breda mechanical industries, it reinforced its position as an economic driving force within Italy and Europe.

In more recent times, Milan has earned its reputation as a global city through its preeminence in various sectors. Home to Italy's stock exchange market Borsa Italiana - it operates as a financial core within Europe while universally recognized labels like Prada, Armani, Dolce & Gabbana hail from Milan's prestigious fashion scene.

Moreover, Milan is renowned for functional yet aesthetic architecture styles fusing modern and historical design, such as the Torre Velasca and CityLife residential towers, which continue to redefine the city's skyline.

Culturally, Milan has always been a melting pot of diverse influences - from Roman antiquity to the creative minds of da Vinci and Verdi. The city's impressive array of historical landmarks, such as Teatro alla Scala, Milan Cathedral (Duomo), and Sforza Castle, stand testament to its rich heritage.

With its deep-rooted history spanning multiple spheres and eras, Milan stands as a testament to human progress and resilience. It is an emblematic city that harmoniously combines distinct cultural and historical influences to create a vibrant, diverse, and modern metropolis. Milan's impact on Italian and European history, economy, arts, culture, and education is undeniable, making it a crucial destination for those wanting to explore the legacy of human creativity and an exceptional environment.

The thriving and dynamic present of the city, enriched by globally recognized industries such as fashion and design, is the result of centuries-long efforts to shape an always-evolving urban landscape that connects its past and present.

MILAN TRAVEL GUIDE 2023

Exploring The Iconic Landmarks

Milan, the vibrant metropolis of Italy, is home to exquisite art, fashion, and architectural wonders that have inspired generations. This chapter takes you on a journey through six of Milan's most iconic landmarks. Unveil the majestic beauty and history of Milan Cathedral (Duomo di Milano), an awe-inspiring symbol of the city. Explore the rich heritage of Sforza Castle (Castello Sforzesco), a breathtaking fortress with artifacts that narrate its colorful past. Step into the opulent La Scala Opera House (Teatro alla Scala), renowned for its world-class performances and captivating ambiance.

Marvel at Leonardo da Vinci's magnificent Last Supper (Il Cenacolo), a masterpiece that captures a moment in time with unparalleled finesse. Immerse yourself in the serene aura of the Church of San Maurizio al Monastero Maggiore, adorned with striking frescoes that will leave you speechless. And finally, take a leisurely stroll through Galleria Vittorio Emanuele II, a stunning shopping arcade garnished with exceptional architecture and design. Join us as we venture into Milan's heart and unveil its timeless treasures.

MILAN TRAVEL GUIDE 2023

Milan Cathedral (Duomo di Milano)

The Milan Cathedral, or Duomo di Milano, is undoubtedly one of the most iconic landmarks in Italy and a must-see destination for anyone visiting Milan. This breathtaking structure, with its mesmerizing gothic architecture and awe-inspiring size, serves as a testament to the city's rich history and Italian craftsmanship. Here, we will explore the Milan Cathedral's origins, architectural details, and the importance it holds for residents and tourists alike.

The Origins of Duomo di Milano

The construction of the Milan Cathedral began in 1386 under the rule of Gian Galeazzo Visconti, who intended the cathedral to be a symbol of Milan's religious and political might. This massive project was financed by local citizens and took centuries to complete. The cathedral was eventually consecrated in 1418, but various additions and modifications continued until 1965. Today, it stands as the largest church in Italy (excluding Saint Peter's Basilica in Vatican City) and the third largest in Europe.

Gothic Architecture

The stunning gothic architecture of the Milan Cathedral makes it one of the most recognizable structures in the world. The cathedral's façade is adorned with over 3,000 statues depicting saints, prophets, and various biblical figures. The building also features more than 100 spires that soar majestically into the sky. A highlight for visitors is climbing up to the terraces for an up-close look at these architectural marvels while enjoying panoramic views of Milan.

Stained Glass Windows & Duomo's Interior

The vibrant stained-glass windows of Duomo di Milano are some of its most captivating features. In particular, the large window above the apse known as *"Grande Vetrata dell'Abside"* is a true masterpiece. These richly colored windows depict scenes from both the Old Testament and New Testament, adding depth to an already awe-inspiring environment within the cathedral.

Stepping inside the Milan Cathedral, visitors are struck by the vast and intricate interior, characterized by its soaring pillars, delicate arches, and fine marble flooring. Noteworthy sights include the *golden Madonnina statue* atop the highest spire,

St. Bartholomew's statue in bronze by Marco d'Agrate, and the numerous relics of saints housed in ornate sarcophagi.

Galleria Vittorio Emanuele II

Adjacent to the cathedral is the Galleria Vittorio Emanuele II, one of the world's oldest shopping malls. Here visitors can enjoy high-end shopping, fine dining, and a taste of Italian culture. The combination of these two key Milan locales illustrates the impressive fusion of past and present in this vibrant city.

Tips For Visiting

The Milan Cathedral is easily accessible by public transportation and is located at Piazza del Duomo in the heart of Milan. Visitors are required to purchase a ticket for entry, and additional experiences like climbing to the terraces or taking part in specialized guided tours are available at an extra charge.

MILAN TRAVEL GUIDE 2023

Sforza Castle (Castello Sforzesco)

When visiting Milan, one essential destination is the impressive Sforza Castle, locally known as Castello Sforzesco. This magnificent fortress-turned-museum has stood proudly for over six centuries, serving as a constant reminder of the power and elegance that has shaped the city over time.

The Origins of Sforza Castle
The grand construction of Sforza Castle began in the 14th century under the rule of Galeazzo II Visconti. However, it was under Francesco Sforza's reign in 1450 when the castle took on its iconic structure. For many years, it served as a residence for Milan's noble families and later played a crucial role in the city's defense against foreign invasions.

MILAN TRAVEL GUIDE 2023

The Museums and Art Collection

Over time, Castello Sforzesco transformed into a center for art and culture. Today, it houses several museums, each holding remarkable collections encompassing history, art, archaeology, and antique instruments. Among them are the *Museum of Ancient Art (Museo d'Arte Antica),* featuring stunning frescoes by Bramantino; the *Archaeological Museum (Museo Archeologico);* and the *Museum of Musical Instruments (Museo degli Strumenti Musicali),* showcasing beautifully-crafted instruments from centuries past.

Perhaps one of the most notable artworks housed within is Michelangelo's unfinished masterpiece: his last sculpture called *"Pietà Rondanini."* The hauntingly unfinished work captures Mary cradling Jesus after his crucifixion—a testament to the artist's unparalleled skill even in his final years.

Parco Sempione and Surrounding Attractions

After exploring the castle's treasures, head outdoors to wander the beautiful Parco Sempione. This vast park encompasses acres of lush greenery and relaxing pathways, perfect for stretching your legs after visiting the museums inside Castello Sforzesco. Other significant attractions nearby include Arco della Pace, a grand triumphal arch dedicated to the end of Napoleon's rule in Milan, and Arena Civica, an amphitheater that hosts concerts and events throughout the year.

MILAN TRAVEL GUIDE 2023

Tips For Visiting

To truly appreciate Sforza Castle and its museums, plan for at least half a day on your itinerary. Consider purchasing a ticket that grants access to all museums within the complex for an all-inclusive experience. To avoid long waiting times, arrive early in the morning or purchase tickets online before your visit.

Located in Milan's city center, Castello Sforzesco is easily accessible via public transportation. You can reach it using Metro Lines 1 (red) and 2 (green), tram lines 1, 2, 4, and 12, or bus line 58.

MILAN TRAVEL GUIDE 2023

La Scala Opera House (Teatro alla Scala)

One of the most exquisite gems of Milan's cultural scene is the La Scala Opera House, also known as Teatro alla Scala. This renowned opera house was established in 1778 and remains one of the most prestigious and historic venues for opera, ballet, and classical music in the world. La Scala attracts tourists and art enthusiasts from across the globe due to its rich history, stunning architectural beauty, and premier performances. A visit to Milan would not be complete without a tour or attending a show at La Scala.

The Origins of La Scala
The history of La Scala can be traced back to 1776 when the Empress Maria Theresa of Austria granted

permission for a new theater to be built on the former site of the church of Santa Maria della Scala (hence its name). The project's construction was spearheaded by architect Giuseppe Piermarini, who aimed to create an opulent venue dedicated to some of the world's finest performances. Two years later, on August 3rd, 1778, it officially opened with a performance of Antonio Salieri's opera "L'Europa riconosciuta."

Architecture and Design
Boasting Neo-classical style architecture that has been masterfully preserved over time, La Scala continues to impress with its regal appearance both inside and out. The theater's magnificent façade is adorned with ornate columns and sculptures that convey an air of grandeur only expected from iconic landmarks.

Upon entering La Scala, visitors will find themselves in the theater's impressive auditorium lined with plush velvet seats and intricate stucco decorations. No detail goes unnoticed as even the chandelier hanging from the ceiling is an awe-inspiring piece crafted from Bohemian crystal. The horseshoe-shaped seating arrangement is designed to optimize acoustics, ensuring every audience member enjoys an unparalleled listening experience.

Legendary Performances and Artists
Over its long and storied history, La Scala has nurtured the talents of prominent artists, composers, conductors, and performers in the world of opera.

Legends like Giuseppe Verdi, Gioachino Rossini, and Arturo Toscanini have graced the stages of La Scala with their presence. To this day, it remains an essential launching platform for opera singers and classical music performers looking to make their mark on the global stage.

The La Scala Museum

For those who wish to delve deeper into the theater's history or appreciate its architecture without attending a performance, a visit to the La Scala Museum is highly recommended. Situated within the theater building, this museum is home to a vast collection of artifacts and documents related to opera and ballet. Visitors can appreciate original manuscripts of famous composers, impressive stage costumes worn by legends like Callas and Caruso, and even an array of rare musical instruments.

Tips For Visiting

To enrich your experience at La Scala, consider taking a guided tour or attending a performance. Both offer unique opportunities to absorb the delicate beauty and unmatched acoustics that make this opera house one of Italy's crown jewels.

Leonardo da Vinci's Last Supper (Il Cenacolo)

Leonardo da Vinci's acclaimed masterpiece, "The Last Supper" or "Il Cenacolo" in Italian, is an exceptional monument that has stood the test of time. It remains one of the most extraordinary and mesmerizing works of art to visit in Milan. Captivating and enthralling, this significant artwork presents a unique insight into the life and mind of one of the greatest minds in history.

Situated in the heart of Milan, The Last Supper is conveniently located at the Convent of Santa Maria delle Grazie. A gem of Renaissance architecture, the church itself holds immense artistic and historical value apart from housing the iconic mural.

The Origins of Leonardo da Vinci's Last Supper

The *"Last Supper"* was commissioned by *Ludovico Sforza*, Duke of Milan, and created between 1495 and 1498. Depicting Christ's last meal with his disciples before his crucifixion, Leonardo's portrayal embraces a wealth of emotions masterfully captured through his intricate brush strokes. The real charm lies in its unique perspective and minute details that warrant a significant portion of your Milan travel itinerary.

For centuries, this monumental fresco has played a crucial role in influencing and shaping Western art. Leonardo da Vinci's innovative conventions and techniques have become iconic in their own right. Even today, many artists look to "The Last Supper" as a supreme example of dramatic storytelling through visual artistry.

Preservation Efforts

After surviving countless wars, environmental deterioration, carelessness from past restorations, and even WWII bombings – The Last Supper still stands as an awe-inspiring tribute to Leonardo's mastery. Ongoing efforts have ensured its preservation for future generations to appreciate this historic piece.

Tips For Visiting

Due to its popularity and significance, obtaining tickets for The Last Supper can be difficult, especially during peak seasons. However, planning ahead and booking in advance will guarantee your visit to this must-see attraction.

Numerous guided tours provide expert historical and artistic knowledge, ensuring you receive an in-depth understanding of the masterpiece and its creator. We highly recommend these tours for keen enthusiasts since limited viewing time is allotted for individual visits.

MILAN TRAVEL GUIDE 2023

Church of San Maurizio al Monastero Maggiore

Nestled in the heart of the bustling city of Milan, the Church of San Maurizio al Monastero Maggiore offers a tranquil oasis that showcases a stunning display of artistic and architectural beauty. Often referred to as *"The Sistine Chapel of Milan," this* hidden gem is a must-visit destination for any admirer of art, history, or religion.

The Origins of Church of San Maurizio al Monastero Maggiore

Founded in the early 16th century, the Church of San Maurizio al Monastero Maggiore was originally part of a monastery complex that was later destroyed during the Napoleonic era. Surviving these tumultuous times, the church has since been preserved and restored, offering visitors a step back into the past.

Designed by Giovanni Antonio Amadeo in the Romanesque style during the early 16th century, this beautiful church features a striking façade with intricate decorations. The bell tower, *Torre della Monachella,* stands out with its delicate style, providing an excellent example of Lombard Renaissance architecture. A unique feature in this Romanesque-Byzantine styled church is the partition wall that separates it into two sections: one for worshippers and one reserved exclusively for the Benedictine nuns.

MILAN TRAVEL GUIDE 2023

Sacred Frescoes

The interior of San Maurizio al Monastero Maggiore is adorned with mesmerizing frescoes that dominate every available inch of wall space. Painted by *Bernardino Luini and his pupils* between 1521 and 1529, these frescoes depict scenes from the New Testament, including *The Last Supper* and *The Crucifixion*. They also showcase several prominent saints' lives, such as Saint Catherine and Saint Agnes. The luminous colors and vivid details offer an awe-inspiring experience for visitors and admirers alike.

The Nuns' Hall

Connected to the main church is a separate hall once reserved for nuns attending Mass. This intimate space overflows with rich spiritual energy. Notable works in this area include an altar by Il Morazzone and an organ dating from 1554. To appreciate this hall's full beauty and serenity, spend some time lingering in this room.

Organ Music

Music enthusiasts should make sure to appreciate the historic organ that presides over the nave. Dating back to 1554 and built by Gerolamo da Romano, this remarkable instrument has undergone various restorations throughout centuries, and its rich, resonant sound can be heard during special events and concerts.

Archeological Finds

Just behind the church, don't miss the chance to visit the Civic Archaeological Museum of Milan. As part of the former monastery complex, this museum boasts a vast collection of Egyptian artifacts, Etruscan inscriptions, and Roman sculptures. If history is your passion, this museum is a must-see during your time in Milan.

Tips For Visiting

Located at Corsa Magenta 15, the church is reachable from Cadorna Railway Station or by using Tram Line 2. Wheelchair accessibility is provided, ensuring everyone has the opportunity to witness this stunning masterpiece.

The Church of San Maurizio al Monastero Maggiore is open daily to visitors, from Tuesday to Sunday, 9.30 AM to 5.30 PM (closed on Mondays). Admission is free, but donations are highly appreciated for maintaining this masterpiece.

For a comprehensive understanding of the Church's artworks and history, consider joining a guided tour. Several companies offer informative tours led by experienced guides who can unravel the mysteries hidden within the enchanting frescoes and share little-known facts about the Church.

Galleria Vittorio Emanuele II

Galleria Vittorio Emanuele II is a must-see destination when visiting Milan. The elegant architecture, excellent shopping options, delectable dining choices, and robust cultural events make this grand arcade one of the city's most treasured landmarks.

The Origins, Architecture, and Design
Inaugurated in 1877, it was designed by architect Giuseppe Mengoni as a symbol of modernity and unity for the recently unified Italian kingdom. The galleria stands proudly with its awe-inspiring glass and iron dome, four-story neoclassical arcade, and imposing triumphal arch entrance.

The architecture is a seamless blend of elegance and grandiosity. The floor is decorated with intricate mosaics representing four continents: Europe, America, Asia, and Africa. The Octagon lies at the center of the galleria with its extraordinary dome soaring above. As you visit this architectural marvel, take a moment to admire its beautiful design and appreciate its rich history.

Shopping Experience

As you enter Galleria Vittorio Emanuele II, you'll find yourself immersed in an exquisite shopping experience that caters to all tastes. It houses a range of high-profile luxury brands such as Prada, Versace, Gucci, Louis Vuitton, along with fashionable Italian designers like Felisi and La Martina. It's not only about fashion; find exquisite gift ideas from high-end bookstores like Libreria Bocca or purchase artistic perfumes from Santa Maria Novella.

Dining Options

Beyond shopping, the galleria offers a wide variety of dining options for every palate. Be sure to visit the historic Camparino bar for an aperitivo – a quintessential Milanese tradition. Enjoy an espresso at Caffè Miani Zucca in Galleria or indulge in fine dining cuisine at Cracco Ristorante; this chic eatery offers delicious Italian fares.

Cultural Events

Galleria Vittorio Emanuele II frequently hosts cultural exhibitions and events, such as fashion shows and art installations that make it an essential part of Milan's vibrant scene. Be sure to check out the schedule for upcoming events while planning your visit.

MILAN TRAVEL GUIDE 2023

Tips For Visiting

Before entering the galleria, it is customary to spin your heel on the bull mosaic located in the center of the floor. This practice is said to bring good luck, and you'll find many visitors participating in this local tradition. Remember to dress appropriately, as you will be visiting a high-end location with luxurious boutiques and top-tier dining establishments. Also, be mindful of pickpockets, as crowded tourist spots can attract them. Finally, don't forget your camera – Galleria Vittorio Emanuele II offers plenty of perfect photo opportunities for unforgettable memories.

MILAN TRAVEL GUIDE 2023

Art And Culture in Milan

Art and culture have always been an integral part of Milan, a vibrant city that pays tribute to its rich history and embraces the contemporary. In this chapter, we will delve into two of Milan's most iconic cultural landmarks, set to inspire any art enthusiast.

Brera Art Gallery (Pinacoteca di Brera)

Milan's rich history and vibrant cultural scene are perhaps best encapsulated in its renowned *Brera Art Gallery (Pinacoteca di Brera),* a must-visit destination for art enthusiasts and casual visitors alike. Here we will delve into the background and significance of the gallery, highlight some key works of art, and give you helpful tips for making the most of your visit.

MILAN TRAVEL GUIDE 2023

Background And History

The Brera Art Gallery finds its roots in the 18th century when it was established by Empress Maria Theresa of Austria as a hub for artistic excellence. Over time, it has evolved into an iconic symbol of Milan's cultural importance and boasts an unrivaled collection of Italian Renaissance masterpieces. Housed within the historic Palazzo di Brera complex, a picturesque setting that is also home to the Brera Library, Botanical Garden, and Astronomical Observatory, the gallery seamlessly fits into this humble abode of knowledge and beauty.

Highlights of Art Collection

Spread across various rooms, categorized by period and style, the art gallery features an impressive collection that will leave you in awe. Among the countless works on display are those by prominent Italian artists such as Raphael, Caravaggio, Tintoretto, Fra Angelico, as well as international painters like Rembrandt and Peter Paul Rubens. Below are several noteworthy masterpieces:

1. "Supper at Emmaus" by Caravaggio - This painting showcases a defining moment from Christ's life following his resurrection when he dines with two disciples at Emmaus. Caravaggio's unrivaled command over light and shadow is brilliantly displayed in this masterpiece.

2. "Marriage of the Virgin" by Raphael - Painted before his 21st birthday while in Florence, this work captures the moment when Mary's hand is symbolically tied to St. Joseph's with a ring. The vibrant color palette and natural composition offer a glimpse into the genius that was Raphael.

3. "Madonna and Child with Two Angels" by Fra Angelico – A timeless classic, this work portrays the Virgin Mary cradling the baby Jesus, surrounded by angels. The ethereal quality of the scene underscores Fra Angelico's unique talent for evoking emotion and spirituality.

4. "The Last Supper" by Andrea Solario - This vivid portrayal of Christ's final meal with his disciples is a striking contrast to Leonardo's more famous version. Notice the detailed expressions of each figure, as well as the dramatic use of light and shadow to create depth in the painting.

Tips for Visiting
1. Plan your visit: Brera Art Gallery is open Tuesday to Sunday from 8.30 AM to 7.15 PM (last admission at 6.40 PM). To avoid long queues and possible delays in entry, it is advisable to book your ticket online in advance. The gallery remains closed on Mondays, December 25th, January 1st, and May 1st.

2. Guided Tours: To maximize your understanding of the collection and its historical value, consider booking a guided tour. These tours are led by knowledgeable experts who can provide fascinating insights into the various works on display.

3. Visit Brera District: Make sure to allocate time to explore the charming Brera District surrounding the gallery – it is one of Milan's most picturesque neighborhoods and a feast for the eyes with its cobbled streets, artisan boutiques, cafés, and restaurants.

4. Audio Guides: For a self-guided experience with supplementary factual information, rent an audio guide available at the gallery entrances in multiple languages.

5. Accessibility: The gallery is wheelchair accessible with ramps at workshops/exhibit rooms entrances and an elevator to all floors; restroom facilities for people using wheelchairs are also available. Moreover, guided tours for visitors with visual impairments can be arranged upon request.

The Brera Art Gallery stands as a proud testament to Milan's exceptional artistic heritage and is an essential destination for anyone who values art, history, and timeless beauty. Be sure to include this astonishing venue on your Milan travel itinerary, and as you wander through its rooms filled with breathtaking artworks, take a moment to appreciate the tremendous talent that has shaped Italy's extraordinary cultural legacy.

Museum of the Twentieth Century (Museo del Novecento)

The Museum of the Twentieth Century, or Museo del Novecento in Italian, is an essential stop for art enthusiasts visiting Milan. This remarkable museum showcases a superb collection of twentieth-century Italian art, covering movements like Futurism, Spatialism, Arte Povera, and many more. In this section, we will delve deeper into the museum's rich history and vast collection, outline the key highlights that you should not miss during your visit, and share some practical tips to make your experience unforgettable.

Background And History
The Museo del Novecento is housed in Palazzo dell'Arengario, a modernist building designed by architects Portaluppi, Magistretti, and Griffini in the 1930s. Before becoming an art museum in 2010, it served various purposes, including hosting a few exhibitions and city offices.

Home to more than 400 artworks spanning the 20th century, the museum encompasses several art movements such as Futurism, Spatialism, Arte Povera, and Italian Pop Art. Its collection boasts pieces by renowned Italian artists like Umberto Boccioni, Amedeo Modigliani, Lucio Fontana, and Giorgio de Chirico.

Key Art Movements Represented
As you explore Museo del Novecento, you will encounter several landmark artistic movements that left an indelible impact on both Italian and international culture.

a) Futurism: Often considered Italy's most vital contribution to twentieth-century art, the Futurism movement celebrated speed, technology, and modernity. The museum showcases influential works by leaders of this movement like Umberto Boccioni, Carlo Carrà, and Giacomo Balla.

b) Metaphysical Painting: With dreamlike scenes and enigmatic symbols, metaphysical painting sought to express a sense of mystery beyond our everyday reality. The work of Giorgio de Chirico features prominently in this section.

c) Abstract Art: Breaking away from traditional representations, abstract artists explored purely formal elements to evoke emotion and meaning. Browse through works by renowned Italian artists like Lucio Fontana and Alberto Burri.

Highlights of the Collection

Museo del Novecento is home to some of twentieth-century Italy's most important art pieces. Among them, a few prominent masterpieces should not be missed:

1. Umberto Boccioni's "Unique Forms of Continuity in Space": A striking bronze sculpture that embodies the principles of the Futurism movement.

2. Giorgio de Chirico's "Melancholy and Mystery of a Street": An iconic work that exemplifies the metaphysical painting style, with its eerie atmosphere and intriguing composition.

MILAN TRAVEL GUIDE 2023

3. **Piero Manzoni's provocative "Artist's Breath,"** which serves as a thought-provoking statement on artistic value and significance.

Tips For Visiting

1. Timings and tickets: The museum is open from Monday to Sunday, except on Tuesdays when it's closed. Ticket prices for adults are €8 (full) and €6 (reduced), while children under 18 enter free of charge. We recommend booking tickets online in advance to avoid disappointment.

2. Guided tours: For a more in-depth understanding of the collection, visitors can join one of the museum's guided tours offered in Italian or English. Tours can be booked in advance on the museum's website or at the ticket desk. These tours are available on Saturdays at 3:00 PM, lasting approximately 90 minutes, and cost an additional €6 per person.

3. Audio guides: If you prefer self-guided exploration, consider renting an audio guide for €5. These guides offer information about museum highlights in Italian, English, French, German and Spanish.

4. MilanoCard holder benefits: Visitors holding a MilanoCard can take advantage of free entry to the Museo del Novecento and other museums throughout Milan.

5. Accessibility: The museum is wheelchair accessible with ramps, elevators, and restrooms specially designed for easy access.

6. Dining Options: If hunger strikes during your visit or if you seek respite from your tour, head over to the ninth floor where you'll find Terrazza Triennale - Osteria con Vista. This contemporary eatery offers delectable Italian cuisine with fantastic views of the Milano Duomo and surrounding area.

7. Night openings: The museum stays open until 10:30 PM on Thursdays and Saturdays. This is an excellent opportunity for visitors looking to enjoy the art in a calmer, more relaxed atmosphere.

No trip to Milan would be complete without visiting the Museum of the Twentieth Century (Museo del Novecento), a treasure trove of modern and contemporary Italian art. As you explore its vast collection, admire the architectural beauty of Palazzo dell'Arengario while immersing yourself in the rich tapestry of Italy's artistic legacy.

MILAN TRAVEL GUIDE 2023

Design And Fashion Districts

In this chapter, we explore Milan's top design and fashion hubs: *Quadrilatero della Moda, Brera Design District, and Porta Nuova District*. Delve into their histories, vibrant atmospheres, and unique characteristics that have made them the epicenters of style and creativity in Italy's bustling metropolis. Discover chic boutiques, innovative galleries, and iconic landmarks as we journey through the city's fashionable enclaves.

Quadrilatero della Moda

The *Quadrilatero della Moda*, also known as *Milan's Fashion District*, is an upscale shopping area where

MILAN TRAVEL GUIDE 2023

the world's most revered luxury brands have made their home. Nestled in the heart of the city, this iconic district boasts a network of four streets - Via Montenapoleone, Via della Spiga, Via Manzoni and Corso Venezia – that create a stylish shopper's paradise.

Discover Milan's High Fashion Scene

The fashion scene in Milan is truly unmatched. As you traverse the Quadrilatero della Moda, prepare to be mesmerized by eye-catching window displays showcasing famed brands like *Prada, Gucci, Dolce & Gabbana, Versace,* and more. Alongside these powerhouses of luxury fashion are accomplished designers and boutiques redefining contemporary style with their innovative creations.

Explore Historical Stores

History and fashion blend seamlessly within the Quadrilatero della Moda. Acquire tailored suits from *Larusmiani* or stroll through iconic establishments like *Pasticceria Cova*– which dates back to 1817 – to indulge in delicious Italian sweets.

Savor Fine Dining Experiences

No trip to the fashion district would be complete without savoring some fine dining experiences. From *Michelin*-starred restaurants to delightful cafes offering traditional Italian cuisine, the possibilities for gastronomic delight are endless. Enjoy a leisurely lunch at *Bagutta* or treat yourself to exquisite Mediterranean dishes at *Il Salumaio di Montenapoleone.*

MILAN TRAVEL GUIDE 2023

Shop Tax-Free for Non-European Union Tourists

Non-European Union tourists can indulge in tax-free shopping at select stores within the Quadrilatero della Moda – perfect for snagging luxury items at competitive prices. Ensure you carry a valid passport and request a tax-free form during checkout. Keep receipts and required documents handy for Customs verification at the airport.

Visit Fashion Museums and Galleries

If the glitz of window-shopping isn't enough, immerse yourself in the rich culture of fashion by visiting nearby museums and galleries. The Armani Silos showcases Giorgio Armani's impressive legacy, while Museo Bagatti Valsecchi offers a glimpse into a historic Milanese home adorned with fine art and lavish antiques.

Tips for Visiting

1. Shops open around 10 AM, with a few boutiques opening later during weekends.
2. Be prepared for shops to close between 2-4 PM as Milan observes the tradition of riposo.
3. Dress codes are more relaxed in the Quadrilatero della Moda; however, ensure you look chic to blend in with Milan's fashionable crowd.
4. Public transport is readily available to access the fashion district; consider using the metro, tram or bus to reach your destination.

The Quadrilatero della Moda is a must-visit destination for any discerning traveler seeking to experience the best of Milan's high fashion and luxury lifestyle. This enthralling district offers an unforgettable melange of historical sites, breathtaking architecture, world-class shopping, and delectable dining experiences.

Brera Design District

The Brera Design District is a vibrant and bustling area filled with art, culture, and creativity. Named after its flagship institution, the *Accademia di Belle Arti di Brera*, this trendy district boasts an eclectic array of art galleries, design shops, museums, and fashionable cafes that will inspire you through every turn.

The Pinacoteca di Brera

No visit to the Brera Design District would be complete without exploring the Pinacoteca di Brera – a world-class art museum housed inside a beautiful 17th-century palace. This revered collection features works by Italian and international artists, such as *Caravaggio, Bellini, Raphael, Rubens, Hayez,* and *Mantegna*. Make sure to allocate at least two hours for your visit to fully appreciate the museum's rich offerings. Admission is free on the first Sunday of each month.

The Botanical Garden of Brera

Adjacent to the Pinacoteca di Brera lies a hidden gem – the *Orto Botanico di Brera* – an urban oasis showcasing a variety of plants from across Italy since 1774. Spread across 5,000 square meters, this lush retreat is an ideal spot to relax and recharge during your time in the district. Don't miss their rare collection of medicinal plants that date back to the Napoleonic era.

Art Galleries in Brera
Renowned for its creative flair, Brera is teeming with boutique art galleries that showcase both established and emerging artists. Must-visit spaces include the *Galleria Giovanni Bonelli, Galleria Carla Sozzani,* and *Galleria Massimo Minini.* Be sure to check their schedules for special events and exhibitions during your stay. Watch out for a variety of free entry shows and openings.

Shopping in Brera
The Brera Design District offers a perfect blend of modernity and tradition. Wander the picturesque streets to discover trendy design shops, such as *OBJECTS by Republic of Fritz Hansen, Alessi,* and *Kartell.* Don't forget to explore the colorful Corso Garibaldi for artisanal crafts, such as ceramics, woodcarvings, and textiles. Spend some time browsing the district's weekend flea market for unique and affordable finds.

Dining in Brera
A day spent exploring the district would be incomplete without indulging in its culinary scene. Savor delicious meals at establishments like *Obicà Mozzarella Bar Brera,* where you can sample an assortment of mozzarella cheeses sourced from southern Italy or cosy trattorias like *La Tartina,* famous for its traditional Italian fare with a modern

twist. Make sure to book ahead during peak mealtimes; many popular eateries fill up quickly!

Fashion and Design in Brera

Lastly, immerse yourself in Brera's array of contemporary fashion and design boutiques showcasing Italian craftsmanship. Highlights include 10 Corso Como - Milan's iconic concept store focused on fashion, design, and art - along with niche brands like Pretziada that combines Sardinian craftsmanship with modern design. Plan your visit during Milan Design Week (Salone del Mobile) or Milan Fashion Week to experience limited-edition installations and events throughout the district.

Tips for Visiting

1. Brera Design Week: Plan your visit during the annual Milan Design Week, typically held in April, to witness the Brera Design District come to life with innovative exhibits, installations, and workshops related to cutting-edge design and architecture.

2. Wear comfortable shoes: As you walk around the cobblestone streets and hidden courtyards of Brera, be sure to wear comfortable shoes to avoid discomfort or injury.

3. Visit during weekdays: Like many other popular Milan attractions, Brera can become quite crowded on weekends. Visiting on a weekday helps ensure a more tranquil and enjoyable experience.

4. Stay nearby: To fully immerse yourself in the vibrant atmosphere of the Brera Design District, consider booking accommodation within the area. There are several boutique hotels and Airbnb options available that cater to various budgets.

5. Guided tours: For an in-depth introduction to the world of design, art, and architecture within Brera Design District, consider joining a guided tour. These tours offer access to exclusive locations and enlightening experiences led by local experts.

MILAN TRAVEL GUIDE 2023

Milanese Cuisine and Local Delicacies

Explore the finest restaurants and authentic street food experiences Milan has to offer. Steeped in culinary history, become acquainted with Milanese specialties that tantalize your taste buds. Uncover the hidden gems and gastronomic wonders sprinkled across this bustling Italian metropolis. Buon appetito!

Traditional Dishes and Where to Find Them

Milan is a city filled with elegance, sophistication and exquisite tastes. The region's culinary delights are considered as benchmarks of Italian cuisine. As you

MILAN TRAVEL GUIDE 2023

explore the depths of this beautiful city, indulge your taste buds in the tantalizing flavors of Milan's traditional dishes, many of which have been passed down through generations.

Risotto alla Milanese

A Milanese staple, Risotto alla Milanese is a delightful creamy dish made with Arborio rice, saffron, onion, white wine, and Parmesan cheese. The golden hue and unique aroma come from the saffron used in the recipe.

Recommended locations:

- *Ristorante Galleria:* Located in the heart of the city, this quaint restaurant offers a decadent take on Risotto alla Milanese.

- *Osteria Del Binari:* This rustic eatery in Via Tortona creates a rich and creamy version that is worth savouring.

Cotoletta alla Milanese

This dish might seem similar to Austrian Wiener Schnitzel. It is made by breading a juicy veal chop and frying it to golden perfection in butter. The crispy crust on the outside contrasts with the tender meat inside.

Recommended locations:

- *Da Martino:* With its history dating back to 1948, Da Martino is renowned for its Cotoletta alla Milanese.

- *Trattoria del Nuovo Macello:* Nestled in Porta Vittoria neighborhood, this trattoria takes pride in offering a succulent version of this iconic dish.

Ossobuco

Ossobuco translates to "bone with a hole". It's a classic Italian stew made from cross-cut veal shanks braised with vegetables, white wine, and broth. The marrow in the bone is a delicacy, making this dish an indulgent experience.

Recommended locations:

- *Osteria del Treno:* Known for its attentive service and home-style cooking, this eatery serves an authentic ossobuco.

- *Antica Trattoria della Pesa:* Located close to Brera, the restaurant has been serving splendid ossobuco since 1880.

Cassoeula

A perfect winter comfort food, cassoeula is made from pork meat and cabbage simmered until tender. The dish has humble origins but a rich flavor profile that has won the hearts of Milanese locals and visitors alike.

Recommended locations:

- *La Pobbia 1850:* One of the oldest trattorias in Milan, La Pobbia 1850 offers traditional cassoeula with genuine flavors.

- *Trattoria Montina:* This family-run restaurant near Porta Romana is ideal for tasting their version of hearty cassoeula.

Panettone

No visit to Milan is complete without trying panettone. This sweet, cake-like bread filled with candied fruits and raisins is popular during Christmas but can be enjoyed at any time of the year.

Recommended locations:

- *Pasticceria G. Cova & C.:* Established in 1817, this pastry shop offers artisanal panettone crafted with high-quality ingredients.

- *Peck:* Known for gourmet food products such as meats, cheeses, and sweets, Peck also showcases delectable panettone.

Gelato

An Italian classic dessert, gelato is a denser yet creamier variant of ice cream. No matter the weather or season, gelato is a must when in Milan.

Recommended locations:

- *CioccolatItaliani:* Located near Duomo di Milano, this popular gelateria offers innovative gelato flavours coupled with rich chocolate.

- *Gelato Giusto:* For classic artisanal gelato made with natural ingredients, head to Via San Gregorio.

As you stroll the streets of Milan, discover these dishes and immerse yourself in the vibrant food culture the city has to offer. From family-run trattorias to chic and modern cafes, experience the range of flavors and traditions ingrained in the rich and diverse Milanese culinary landscape. Enjoy every bite and let Milan reveal its enticing secrets one dish at a time.

Best Restaurants & Street Food Experiences

With a perfect blend of traditional Italian flavors and modern international cuisine, the Milan's dining options are nothing short of spectacular. In this section, we will explore some of the best restaurants and street food experiences that Milan has to offer. So, buckle up and prepare your taste buds for a gastronomic adventure!

MILAN TRAVEL GUIDE 2023

Trattoria della Pesa

One of the oldest and most iconic trattorias in Milan, Trattoria della Pesa is known for its traditional Milanese dishes. Nestled in a beautiful historic building, this cozy restaurant offers delectable treats like Osso Buco (veal shanks braised with vegetables) and Risotto alla Milanese (saffron-infused risotto). Don't forget to pair your meal with one of their exquisite local wines to complete your experience.

Ratana

Rooted in sustainability and regional ingredients, Ratana offers a contemporary take on Lombardy's culinary traditions. Located in an early 20th-century building, the minimalist interiors create an elegant atmosphere that complements its creative menu. Highlights include the Tonno di coniglio (rabbit prepared like tuna) and Cotoletta alla Milanese (breaded veal cutlet). Their seasonal offerings add freshness to an already exciting menu.

Piz

Milan may not be as famous for pizza like Naples is, but Piz stands out from the rest with their focus on quality ingredients and authentic flavors. From the classics such as Margherita and Diavola to more unique offerings incorporating truffle or burrata cheese, you'll find intriguing combinations to satisfy any palate. Their minimalist interior sets your focus squarely on their mouthwatering pizzas.

MILAN TRAVEL GUIDE 2023

Ristorante Cracco

For a fine dining experience in Milan, Ristorante Cracco is a must-visit. Helmed by renowned Chef Carlo Cracco, the restaurant is housed within the stylish Galleria Vittorio Emanuele II shopping arcade. The culinary journey here is nothing short of extraordinary, starting with house-made bread and continuing through elaborate courses featuring seafood, meat, and pasta. It's not surprising that Ristorante Cracco boasts two Michelin stars.

Now that we've visited some exceptional restaurants let's delve into Milan's fascinating street food scene! The streets are filled with countless vendors offering delicious bites for you to enjoy on the go.

Luini Panzerotti

No visit to Milan would be complete without trying panzerotti at Luini Panzerotti, located just around the corner from Piazza San Babila. These deep-fried pockets of heavenly dough come filled with a variety of ingredients like mozzarella and tomato, spicy salami, or vegetables. Prepared fresh daily, they are the perfect snack or light meal while exploring the city.

La Dogana del Buongusto

This modern delicatessen serves up an array of mouthwatering sandwiches filled with authentic Italian cold cuts and cheeses. While you can't go wrong with anything on their menu, their mozzarella stuffed with truffles or selection of locally sourced salamis are particularly outstanding. Enjoy your sandwich on one of their outdoor tables for a relaxed al-fresco meal.

Pave Gelateria

Treat yourself to some artisan gelato at Pave Gelateria in the heart of the lively Porta Venezia neighborhood. With an array of flavors that vary seasonally as well as some intriguing combinations such as ricotta & figs or melon & prosciutto, your taste buds will be in for a delightful experience. Don't forget to end your day of gastronomic exploration by indulging in this creamy masterpiece.

The food scene in Milan offers a plethora of unmissable experiences, from high-end dining establishments to casual street food joints. Whatever your culinary preferences might be, this city promises to leave you satisfied and inspired. As a traveler, it's essential to not only explore the beautiful streets and architecture of Milan but also to embrace its vibrant and diverse gastronomic culture. Buon appetito!

MILAN TRAVEL GUIDE 2023

Insider Tips from Locals

This chapter is your ultimate guide to discovering the hidden gems, unknown spots, and authentic neighborhoods of this charming Italian city. As you explore the vibrant streets of Milan, you'll not only discover its renowned landmarks but also unveil secret nooks and crannies unknown to many tourists.

We will share with you some remarkable hidden gems and lesser-known attractions that are worth exploring. Moreover, we will guide you through recommended neighborhoods where locals love to hang out, savor delectable cuisine, and experience the genuine Milanese way of life. Get ready to uncover extraordinary surprises awaiting you in enchanting Milan.

Hidden Gems and Lesser-Known Local Attractions

While the iconic landmarks such as the Cathedral of Milan and Galleria Vittorio Emanuele II are definite must-sees on any trip to Milan, there are many hidden gems and lesser-known local attractions that should not be missed. In this section, we will guide you through a selection of these unique experiences, immersing you in the soul of Milan beyond the beaten path.

1. The Secret Garden of Via Lincoln: A peaceful oasis in an urban jungle, the Giardino Segreto di Via

Lincoln lies within a residential courtyard. Entered through a narrow passageway and shrouded by nature, this botanical refuge boasts an impressive collection of plants that thrive amongst classical sculptures and serene fountains.

2. Villa Necchi Campiglio: This elegant residence turned museum offers an insight into the lifestyle of an affluent family from the early 20th century. Designed by architect Piero Portaluppi between 1932 and 1935, Villa Necchi Campiglio showcases a blend of Art Deco, Rationalism, and Novecento style. Enjoy guided tours through its preserved interiors or explore its beautiful garden.

4. Quartiere Fiera and Hangar Bicocca: Contemporary art lovers will be drawn to the Hangar Bicocca, a vast, industrial post-modern space. Frequently hosting thought-provoking exhibitions and site-specific installations from some of the world's leading contemporary artists, the Hangar Bicocca is a must-visit for those looking to explore Milan's thriving art scene.

5. Biblioteca della Moda: Nestled in the heart of Milan's fashion district is the Biblioteca della Moda, an extensive archive of fashion literature. With over 70,000 publications that span sustainability initiatives to detailed documentation of renowned fashion shows, this library can quickly transform into a fashion enthusiast's paradise.

6. Biblioteca degli Alberi Milano (BAM): Situated close to Bosco Verticale - yet another architectural marvel of Milan - is Biblioteca degli Alberi Milano (BAM), an urban park filled with green life. Commonly referred to as "The library of trees," BAM houses more than 130 tree species adorned with public art. You'll also find a web of walking and cycling paths - the perfect spot to unwind and enjoy nature.

7. The Church of San Bernardino alle Ossa: Step off the beaten path and catch a glimpse of the macabre at the Church of San Bernardino alle Ossa. Though it may look like any other church from the outside, the ossuary holds an eerie hidden chapel where human bones adorn its walls. Visit this unique place for a chilling historical experience.

8. Frog Ghetto (Quartiere delle Rane): In a quiet residential area, you'll discover Milan's art-enriched Frog Ghetto. Located around Via Padova, this neighborhood is known for its vibrant murals featuring frogs, created by famed street artist Pao. The colorful frogs reflect the creative energy of this otherwise overlooked part of Milan.

9. Legare Café: Legare Café, a true local gem, is situated on picturesque Alzaia Naviglio Grande. Offering fair trade coffee, organic wine, and an abundance of books to lose yourself in, this cozy venue is ideal for travelers seeking solace amidst the city buzz.

10. Pezzi di Vetro: For a taste of vintage clothing and rare antiques, wander into Pezzi di Vetro, a quaint storefront located in the Navigli district. This treasure trove offers an eclectic array of items ranging from fashionable threads to impeccable curios – perfect for those looking to bring back unique souvenirs or gifts.

11. Chiesa di Santa Maria presso San Satiro: Nestled between shops and cafés lies Chiesa di Santa Maria presso San Satiro - an unassuming yet beautiful church known for its architectural trompe-l'oeil by Renaissance artist Bramante. With an illusionary spaciousness that belies its confined quarters, this is an artistic marvel you won't want to miss.

12. Head to Chinatown: Explore Milan's multicultural side in its quaint Chinatown district located near Porta Venezia. With a range of authentic Chinese restaurants, supermarkets, and boutiques, immerse yourself in Eastern culture amidst the backdrop of Italian architecture.

13. Leonardo da Vinci's Vineyard (La Vigna di Leonardo): Within walking distance from the iconic Last Supper painting lies Leonardo da Vinci's Vineyard - a lesser-known but fascinating attraction. Awarded to Leonardo by his patron Ludovico Sforza as payment for creating "The Last Supper," you can explore the carefully restored vineyard along with Casa Degli Atellani – one of the few remaining examples of 15th-century Milanese architecture.

14. Isola and Porta Nuova District: While many tourists focus on central Milan, there are still more gems waiting to be discovered in other areas like Isola and Porta Nuova district. Known for its vibrant street art scene and contemporary buildings such as Bosco Verticale (Vertical Forest), these neighborhoods offer fantastic food options and entertainment experiences that define modern Milan.

15. Torre Branca: Offering panoramic bird's-eye views of Milan, the Torre Branca is an 108.60-meter steel-structured tower situated in the Sempione Park. Although overshadowed by its more famous brother, Torre Velasca, this landmark is an ideal escape from the bustling city and a chance to see Milan from a new perspective.

16. Museo Poldi Pezzoli: This opulent, private museum is often overlooked by tourists but offers an exquisite collection of Renaissance art. A former residence turned museum, Museo Poldi Pezzoli is home to works by Botticelli, Bellini, and Mantegna, among others, with its charming interiors intactly maintaining the original 19th-century layout. It's a great place to discover a lesser-known side of Milan's art scene and marvel at the beautiful decorative arts, including armor, glass, porcelain, and textiles.

17. Go on a scavenger hunt for Giuseppe De Nittis' hidden artworks: In the 1800s, Italian artist Giuseppe De Nittis painted stunning frescoes on shutters that adorn several buildings across the city.

Seek out these hidden works of art and experience Milan from a different perspective.

As you dive deep into Milan's secret corners and hidden gems, embrace the local knowledge we've shared in this section. Be sure to venture off the well-trodden path and seek out these lesser-known attractions for a truly authentic and memorable travel experience in Italy's beautiful metropolis.

Recommended Local Neighborhoods for Exploration

As you dive into the local culture, you'll find that there is more to this city than meets the eye. This section highlights some lesser-known districts within Milan that are perfect for the curious traveler.

1. Navigli District: The Navigli District has a unique charm due to its picturesque network of canals. Leonardo da Vinci himself designed this intricate waterway system during the Renaissance era. Today, it's filled with vibrant bars, delightful boutiques, and art galleries. Don't forget to visit the monthly antique market or take a relaxing evening stroll along the scenic waterfront.

2. Isola District: Welcome to one of Milan's lesser-known gems, the Isola District! This trendy neighborhood has undergone extensive urban renewal projects in recent years, transforming it into a modern hotspot that embraces its historic roots.

Graffiti art by local artists adorns its buildings while offering a revitalizing atmosphere. Visit the stunning architecture of Bosco Verticale and delight your taste buds at local eateries.

3. Brera District: Historically a bohemian haven, Brera retains its artsy atmosphere with numerous small studios and galleries tucked away among its narrow streets. Stop by Pinacoteca di Brera, Milan's principal art gallery that houses an impressive collection of Italian artwork dating back centuries. Wander through lush gardens in Orto Botanico di Brera or sip on an espresso in small hipster cafés.

4. Porta Romana District: Gateway to the Roman Empire era, Porta Romana holds historical significance due to its well-conserved ancient walls. It is now a fashionable residential area which boasts top-rated restaurants and exciting nightlife venues. Grab a cocktail at Viale Montenero or pamper yourself at Terme Milano, a fashionable spa designed for rest and relaxation.

5. Porta Venezia District: Celebrated for its outstanding Art Nouveau architecture, the Porta Venezia neighborhood emanates elegance. Take your time as you meander through the exquisite streets, gazing at the intricately designed balconies and façades before sinking into the tranquility of Giardini Pubblici Indro Montanelli. The district also accommodates a multicultural presence with numerous international eateries.

6. Chinatown-Milan: While not as expansive as its counterparts in other cities, Milan's Chinatown is a cozy area offering a splendid array of Asian dining options. Walk down Via Paolo Sarpi to find street food vendors selling delectable delights like dim sum and bubble tea to mom-and-pop shops selling traditional Chinese ingredients.

7. Lambrate-Ventura District: This cutting-edge district reflects Milan's dedication to contemporary design and innovation. Each year during the Salone del Mobile, streets transform into exhibition spaces filled with artwork and furniture by up-and-coming designers. Venture into this eclectic district to discover an abundance of contemporary art galleries, unique boutiques, and avant-garde installations.

As you charter your journey across these neighborhoods, keep in mind that Italy's approach to urban planning often prioritizes pedestrians over motor vehicles. As such, exploring on foot or by bike will reward you with unique discoveries while serving as an ode to the city's environmentalist ethos.

These magical pockets within Milan are sure to enchant each traveler with their distinct personalities. From picturesque canals in Navigli to vibrant graffiti in Isola, embrace the opportunity for adventure by uncovering each neighborhood's unique charms and hidden treasures that make them so beloved among locals and visitors alike.

MILAN TRAVEL GUIDE 2023
BOOK 2 // The Italian Lakes

MILAN TRAVEL GUIDE 2023

Introduction to the Italian Lakes Region

Welcome to *"Italian Lakes Region,"* an enchanting journey through Northern Italy's magnificent lakes, each with its unique charm and appeal. In this chapter, we delve into the captivating magic of Lake Como, Lake Garda, Lake Maggiore, and Lake Orta, unraveling their stories, history, and mystique.

Overview of Lake Como, Lake Garda, Lake Maggiore, and Lake Orta

From serene shores to dynamic landscapes, each lake boasts striking geographical features and unparalleled natural beauty that have been cherished by locals and tourists alike for centuries. Nestled between soaring mountains and lush valleys, these mesmerizing lakes form a picturesque backdrop that provides both relaxation and adventure.

Lake Como
Covering an area of approximately 146 square kilometers, Lake Como is renowned for its stunning beauty and dramatic scenery. The lake is shaped like an inverted "Y" with three branches intersecting at the charming town of Bellagio. The lakeside towns are characterized by their colorful houses nestled on the

slopes of green hills that reach down to the water's edge.

One of the main attractions at Lake Como is Villa del Balbianello in Lenno, a magnificent 18th-century villa surrounded by manicured gardens. This historic estate has been featured in numerous films such as Casino Royale and Star Wars Episode II. Another popular destination is the town of Varenna, famous for its picturesque streets and Villa Monastero with its stunning gardens.

The towns around Lake Como provide a variety of accommodation options ranging from luxurious hotels to charming bed and breakfasts. Some suggestions include Grand Hotel Villa Serbelloni in Bellagio or Hotel Du Lac in Varenna.

Lake Garda

The largest Italian lake, Lake Garda covers an area of 370 square kilometers and boasts a diverse landscape with rugged mountains in the north and olive groves in the south. It is well known for its medieval towns and castles dotting its shores.

Sirmione is one of the most visited towns on Lake Garda. This picturesque town is situated on a peninsula and features the stunning Scaligero Castle, Grotte di Catullo Roman ruins, and thermal springs. Another highlight is the town of Malcesine, where you can take a cable car ride up to Monte Baldo for breathtaking panoramic views.

Accommodation options around Lake Garda cater to different preferences, whether you are looking for a serene lakeside retreat or a lively resort. Recommended options include Grand Hotel Fasano in Gardone Riviera or Hotel Castello Lake Front in Malcesine.

Lake Maggiore
Straddling the border between Italy and Switzerland, Lake Maggiore covers an area of about 213 square kilometers. The lake is famous for its Borromean Islands, which consist of Isola Bella, Isola Madre, and Isola dei Pescatori. These islands can be visited by taking a boat tour from Stresa or Baveno.

Isola Bella is home to the magnificent Palazzo Borromeo with its beautifully landscaped gardens featuring fountains, terraces, and statues. Isola Madre houses a botanical garden with exotic plants and a historic villa with a collection of marionettes. Isola dei Pescatori, also known as Fishermen's Island, charms visitors with its quaint village atmosphere and narrow streets lined with restaurants serving fresh seafood.

For accommodations near Lake Maggiore, consider staying at Grand Hotel Des Iles Borromees in Stresa or Villa e Palazzo Aminta Hotel Beauty and Spa in Baveno.

Lake Orta
The smallest among these four lakes, Lake Orta is often considered a hidden gem with its relaxed

atmosphere and charming towns. The main town on the lake is Orta San Giulio with its medieval center and stunning views of the island of San Giulio.

A visit to the Sacro Monte di Orta, a UNESCO World Heritage site located on a hilltop above the town, provides unique insights into Italian art and religion. The site features 20 chapels with frescoes and terracotta sculptures depicting the life of St. Francis of Assisi.

While Lake Orta offers fewer accommodation options than the other lakes, some choices include Hotel San Rocco in Orta San Giulio or Villa Crespi, a luxurious hotel housed in a 19th-century Moorish-style mansion.

In conclusion, the four Italian lakes near Milan each offer distinct attractions and enchanting landscapes that cater to different tastes and preferences. Whether you prefer the glamour of Lake Como, the diverse scenery of Lake Garda, the cultural offerings of Lake Maggiore, or the relaxation of Lake Orta, the lakes are sure to leave a lasting impression on all who visit them.

From charming towns filled with history and culture to luxurious hotels and breathtaking vistas, you won't want to miss an opportunity to explore these wonders of nature that are just a short train ride away from Milan.

MILAN TRAVEL GUIDE 2023

Geographical Highlights and Natural Beauty

As you explore the Italian Lakes through this Milan Travel Guide, one can't help but marvel at the impeccable blend of stunning geographical highlights and captivating natural beauty that exudes from each body of water. Italy, a nation known for its picturesque landscapes, truly showcases Mother Nature's finest artistry when it comes to the lakes situated within its boundaries.

Geographical Highlights

Situated in the northern parts of Italy and partially extending into Switzerland, the Italian Lakes region is a splendor to behold. Formed primarily by glacial erosion during the last Ice Age, these lakes are nestled among Alpine foothills, which provide stunning backdrops to their expansive waters. The most renowned Italian lakes include Lake Como, Lake Maggiore, Lake Garda, and Lake Orta – each with distinct characteristics worthy of exploration.

1. Lake Como: With an inverted Y shape originating at the town of Colico in the north and resembling two long branches splaying southward toward Lecco and Como cities respectively, Lake Como is a breathtaking sight from any vantage point. Verdant mountain slopes surround its crystal-clear waters, offering panoramic views that will make your heart race with wonder.

2. Lake Maggiore: As Italy's second-largest lake (and straddling Switzerland as well), Lake Maggiore boasts remarkable scenery attributable to its unique geography. With shores that encompass both flatlands and dramatic alpine landscapes, one can expect a diverse fusion of natural wonders in this sublime haven.

3. Lake Garda: The largest lake in Italy, Lake Garda's strikingly diverse environment ranges from idyllic vineyards and olive groves to verdurous hillsides dotted with age-old castles. These diverse geographical elements combine harmoniously to create a picture-perfect landscape for those who seek solace in nature's embrace.

4. Lake Orta: Famed for its congenial atmosphere and astounding beauty on a smaller scale, Lake Orta exudes tranquility amidst its picturesque lakeside villages and densely wooded mountains. The lake acts as a sanctuary for those who crave a quaint and serene escape.

Natural Beauty
The Italian Lakes region is not only known for its stunning geographical features but also holds many secrets that can be unearthed through their natural beauty. With diverse flora and fauna, splendid gardens, and enchanting secluded spots – the Italian Lakes seem to continually unveil hidden gems for the discerning traveler.

1. **Flora and Fauna:** Each Italian Lake is blessed with distinct flora and fauna that burst to life each season. From endemic fish species to migratory birds that seek refuge along the lakes' shores, both nature enthusiasts and casual observers will find wonder in the delicate ecosystems encompassing these pristine waters.

2. **Gardens and Parks:** Nurtured by the gentle Mediterranean climate, the Italian Lakes are home to many majestic gardens and parks teeming with a wide array of botanical wonders. Notable gardens like Isola Bella on Lake Maggiore, Villa Carlotta on Lake Como, Heller Garden on Lake Garda, and Villa Romantica on Lake Iseo boast vibrant floral displays that captivate visitors with their striking seasonal colors.

3. **Secluded Spots:** The Italian Lakes region doesn't lack romantic nooks or peaceful places where travelers can find solace away from bustling town centers. Each lake features serene walks along waterfront promenades or secluded bays accessible by boat. Alternatively, venture into nearby forests or hillside trails to uncover seemingly untouched corners of this land, allowing you to appreciate nature's grandeur undisturbed.

In closing, the enchanting Italian Lakes reveal themselves in more ways than one – from jaw-dropping geographical attributes to their abounding natural beauty. The lakes offer a medley of captivating treasures awaiting discovery for those keen on immersing themselves within these magical shores.

MILAN TRAVEL GUIDE 2023

Lake Como

Nestled in the picturesque region of Lombardy, Lake Como is a breathtaking destination that has captured the hearts and imaginations of both tourists and locals. In this chapter, we embark on a journey to explore the charming towns and attractions that adorn its shores - from the enchanting Bellagio and Varenna, to the historic Villa del Balbianello and Como. Each town offers its own unique allure, boasting vibrant architecture, age-old traditions, and a standing invitation to an authentic Italian experience.

Beyond its beauty, Lake Como presents a plethora of outdoor activities for everyone. Indulge in water sports, take boat tours, or challenge yourself with exhilarating hiking adventures set against the captivating backdrop. Discover a realm of quintessential Italian charm at the wondrous Lake Como.

Towns and Attractions in Lake Como

Lake Como, affectionately referred to as the *"Pearl of the Italian Lakes,"* has long captivated visitors with its crystal-clear waters, lush scenery, and charming villages. In this chapter, we explore several picturesque towns and attractions around Lake Como that should be on every visitor's itinerary: Bellagio, Varenna, Villa del Balbianello, and the eponymous Como.

Bellagio

Bellagio is a quintessential stop during any visit to Lake Como. This charming town is nestled at the point where the lake divides into two arms, offering breathtaking panoramic views. Wander through its narrow-cobbled streets lined with pastel-colored buildings adorned with lush gardens and beautiful terraces overlooking the calm waters of Lake Como.

One of Bellagio's main attractions is *Villa Melzi*, featuring a neoclassical structure surrounded by impressive English-style gardens with diverse flora from around the world. You can also take a relaxed stroll along *Lungolago Europa*, which runs parallel to the lakeshore and offers remarkable vistas of the surrounding landscape.

MILAN TRAVEL GUIDE 2023

Varenna

The enchanting town of Varenna boasts a romantic atmosphere, thanks to its serene shoreline promenade and historic center filled with captivating alleyways and hidden courtyards. Accessible by both train and boat, Varenna makes for an ideal base for those looking to explore Lake Como.

Begin your visit by meandering through *Varenna's maze-like layout* until you reach the *Church of San Giorgio*. Dating back to 1313, this beautifully preserved church contains valuable artwork from centuries past. Just a short walk along Varenna's waterfront promenade will take you to *Villa Monastero* – a museum housed in an old Cistercian convent. The villa's charming gardens provide beautiful views of Lake Como and make for an idyllic setting in which to relax.

Villa del Balbianello

Although technically situated in Lenno, *Villa del Balbianello* is easily accessible from both Bellagio and Varenna by boat. This stunning 18th-century villa is not only a must-see for its marvelous architecture, but also for its breathtaking garden. Set on a verdant promontory jutting out into the lake, the villa boasts some of the most spectacular views in the region.

Famous for being featured in films such as *Star Wars: Episode II* and *Casino Royale*, Villa del Balbianello is open to the public for guided tours. Soak in its exquisite interiors adorned with artifacts collected by its former owner, Count Guido Monzino – an Italian explorer who reached the summit of Mount Everest in 1973.

Como

The cosmopolitan city of Como sits at the southern end of Lake Como and serves as a gateway to the region. Travelers can reach Como by train or boat and explore its historic center brimming with medieval architecture, fashionable shops, and lively piazzas.

Begin your tour of Como at *Cathedral Santa Maria Assunta (Duomo di Como)*. This grand Gothic-Renaissance edifice is adorned with majestic sculptures and exquisite paintings, making it a masterpiece from both inside and out. Just steps away from the cathedral, be sure to visit *Piazza Cavour* – Como's vibrant main square brimming with bustling restaurants, cafes, and charming boutiques.

No visit to Como would be complete without a trip up to *Brunate* – a picturesque village perched on a hill overlooking Lake Como. Hop aboard the funicular railway that ascends from the city center and enjoy breathtaking views as you climb higher into the clouds. Once at Brunate, reward yourself with a cozy meal at one of their local trattorias before embarking on a leisurely hike through the lush hills.

The towns and attractions in Lake Como hold something for everyone, from lovers of history and culture to those just looking for a breathtaking escape amidst stunning natural beauty. As you explore Lake Como, allow yourself to get lost in the magic of the Pearl of the Italian Lakes and create memories that will last a lifetime.

Water Sports, Boat Tours, and Hiking Opportunities

Apart from its picturesque landscapes and historic villages, Lake Como is an adventure seeker's paradise. This section will explore the many water sports, boat tours, and hiking opportunities that you can enjoy during your stay at this magnificent Italian lake.

Water Sports

1. Kayaking and Canoeing: Paddling through the calm waters of Lake Como is an excellent way to immerse yourself in the lake's serene beauty. Numerous rental companies offer kayaks and canoes for visitors to explore secluded beaches, quiet coves, and waterfront villas along the lake's expansive shoreline.

2. Stand-Up Paddleboarding (SUP): Another popular water activity is stand-up paddleboarding. This sport provides participants with an enjoyable workout while experiencing stunning views of the lake and surrounding mountains. Several rental shops around the lake offer SUP boards and lessons for all experience levels.

3. Windsurfing: Lake Como has consistent winds that make it an ideal location for windsurfing. Enthusiasts can rent equipment and take lessons at various clubs around the lake, such as Colico's Windsurf Center in the northern part of Lake Como.

4. Sailing: For a more leisurely water activity, consider chartering a sailboat or joining a sailing course at one of Lake Como's marinas or clubs like Circolo Vela di Mandello del Lario. Whether you're an experienced sailor or a complete beginner, sailing on Lake Como offers an unforgettable way to soak up its picturesque surroundings.

Boat Tours

1. Private Boat Tours: A private boat tour is an excellent way to discover Lake Como at your own pace while enjoying personalized service from an experienced skipper. Charter a luxury yacht or rent a small motorboat to explore the lake's hidden gems and its world-famous villas like Villa Balbianello and Villa Carlotta.

2. Public Ferry Services: Navigazione Lago di Como is the leading public ferry service that offers several routes along Lake Como, allowing visitors to hop on and off at numerous picturesque towns like Menaggio, Bellagio, and Varenna. The ferries operate regularly throughout the day, providing an affordable and convenient way to explore the area.

3. Fit & Fun Lake Tour: For travelers who prefer a more active approach to sightseeing, the Fit & Fun Lake Tour combines water sports with exploration. Participants paddle between scenic locations on kayaks, canoes, or SUP boards, enjoying guided tours of historic sites and a delightful waterfront lunch.

Hiking Opportunities

1. Greenway del Lago di Como: Stretching over 10km from Colonno in the south to Griante Cadenabbia in the north, the Greenway is a scenic walking path that meanders through picturesque villages, ancient alleyways, and lush landscapes on the lake's western shore. This accessible hike offers stunning panoramic views and ample opportunities for detours to lakeside cafes, secluded beaches, or olive groves.

2. Monte Grona: For a more challenging hike with rewarding panoramic vistas, head to Monte Grona. The summit of this 1,736-meter mountain offers breathtaking views of Lake Como and its surroundings. Several paths lead to the top; however, it is recommended to start your ascent from Breglia – an intermediate-level route.

3. Sentiero del Viandante: Meaning *"the Wanderer's Path,"* the Sentiero del Viandante is a historic trail that runs along the lake's eastern shore from *Abbadia Lariana to Piantedo*. Divided into various stages of difficulty, hikers on this ancient trade route can explore medieval villages, terraced vineyards, chestnut forests, and striking views of the lake.

As you plan your itinerary for your trip to this enchanting Italian destination, be sure to make time

MILAN TRAVEL GUIDE 2023

for these thrilling activities that showcase the unparalleled beauty of Lake Como.

MILAN TRAVEL GUIDE 2023

Lake Garda

Located at the foot of the Italian Alps, Lake Garda is a stunning mix of picturesque towns, breathtaking attractions, and an abundance of outdoor activities. In this chapter, we will guide you through the enchanting towns of Sirmione, with its ancient fortress-like charm, and Malcesine, graced by the magnificent Scaliger Castle. For those seeking thrills and excitement, Gardaland Theme Park offers unforgettable experiences for all ages.

As you explore this haven of beauty, indulge in some of Italy's finest wine-tasting events along the sun-kissed shores, and partake in a myriad of outdoor pursuits that cater to both adrenaline junkies and serenity-seekers alike.

MILAN TRAVEL GUIDE 2023

Towns and Attractions in Lake Garda

Lake Garda, the largest lake in Italy, is a true paradise for tourists and locals alike. Surrounded by picturesque towns and thrilling attractions, it offers something for everyone. In this section, we will take a closer look at some of the most charming towns and exciting attractions around Lake Garda.

Sirmione

Nestled on a peninsula extending into the azure waters of Lake Garda, Sirmione is a picturesque town known for its stunning beauty, rich history, and relaxing thermal baths. The narrow cobblestone streets of Sirmione are lined with colorful houses, inviting cafes, and quaint shops that sell everything from handmade soaps to mouthwatering gelato.

The town's most iconic landmark is the imposing *Scaliger Castle*, boasting an impressive fortress surrounded by a moat. Built in the 13th century by the Scaliger family, this majestic castle once served as a military stronghold and now houses a small museum that showcases the history of Sirmione and its surrounding areas.

A short walk from the castle takes you to *Grotte di Catullo*, an ancient Roman villa dating back to the 1st century AD. The well-preserved ruins offer a fascinating glimpse into the everyday life during Roman times while boasting panoramic views over Lake Garda.

MILAN TRAVEL GUIDE 2023

Malcesine

Located on the eastern shores of Lake Garda and nestled at the foot of Monte Baldo, Malcesine is another enchanting town with narrow winding streets and a rich medieval heritage. This charming town's main attractions include its picturesque harbor lined with vibrant houses and bustling cafes.

The centerpiece of Malcesine is undoubtedly *Castello Scaligero*, another example of Scaliger architecture dating back to the 13th century. The castle towers above Lake Garda, offering breathtaking views of both the lake and *Monte Baldo's* rugged peaks. The castle also houses a museum dedicated to Lake Garda's natural history and the region's folklore.

A cable car ride from the town takes you to the summit of Monte Baldo, where you can experience spectacular views and explore the mountain's diverse flora and fauna. For adventure-seekers, there are several trails for hiking and mountain biking or paragliding opportunities to take flight.

Gardaland Theme Park

For families seeking a fun-filled day out around Lake Garda, a visit to Gardaland Theme Park is an absolute must. As Italy's largest amusement park, it attracts millions of visitors each year and offers a vast array of cxciting rides, attractions, and entertaining shows catering to all ages.

Thrill-seekers will find adrenaline-pumping roller coasters like *Oblivion: The Black Hole*, while younger visitors can enjoy family-friendly attractions such as *Prezzemolo Treehouse* or join *Peppa Pig and Friends* in their adventures. In addition to rides, Gardaland features live shows, colorful parades, and spectacular firework displays in the evenings.

Scaliger Castle

The crowning jewel in Sirmione's skyline is undoubtedly Scaliger Castle. As one of the most well-preserved medieval fortresses in Italy, it stands guard over Lake Garda and bears testament to the power and influence of the Scaligers who once ruled this region.

The castle complex consists of a central keep surrounded by sturdy walls with watchtowers on each corner. Visitors can explore numerous rooms filled with exquisite frescoes depicting scenes from medieval life or head to the top of the main tower for panoramic views over Sirmione and Lake Garda.

Scaliger Castle also hosts temporary exhibitions and special events throughout the year that showcase local art, music, and culture. Don't forget to take a leisurely stroll along its fortified walkways by the lake as you soak in the picturesque surroundings and breathe in the scents of Mediterranean vegetation.

Whether you are visiting Sirmione's historical landmarks, exploring Malcesine's medieval charm, or looking for adrenaline-pumping excitement at

Gardaland Theme Park, this beautiful corner of Italy will leave you captivated and craving to discover more.

Wine Tasting and Outdoor Activities

Lake Garda offers an abundance of outdoor activities and truly unique wine tasting experiences for travelers to enjoy. Here, we will delve into the world of wine tasting on the lake's shores and explore some of the best outdoor experiences Lake Garda has to offer.

Wine Tasting Experiences

The fertile soil and mild Mediterranean climate make the Lake Garda region an ideal place for growing grapes. Vineyards dotted around the lake produce some of Italy's most renowned wines, including Lugana, Bardolino, Valpolicella, and Amarone. Let's explore some top wine tasting destinations in the area.

1. Cà Maiol Winery - Known for their exquisite Lugana wines, Cà Maiol boasts a beautiful estate located in the Desenzano del Garda area. Here, you can taste delicious wines produced from Turbiana grapes while basking in the picturesque views of vineyards and lake.

2. Zeni Wine Museum - Located on a hill overlooking Bardolino town, Zeni Winery offers more than just tastings; it's an immersive experience combining art, history, and oenology. In addition to sampling Zeni's fine Bardolino wines, visitors can learn about winemaking history at their own pace through a self-guided tour of the museum.

3. Tommasi Viticoltori - For fans of bold reds like Amarone and Valpolicella Ripasso, visit Tommasi Viticoltori located in the charming village of Pedemonte. Tommasi has been in operation since 1902 and offers comprehensive guided tours that provide insight into their winemaking process, history, and wine philosophy.

Outdoor Activities

Apart from indulging in wine-tasting experiences, Lake Garda offers an array of outdoor activities ranging from water sports to hiking, cycling, and golf. Here are a few activities to include during your visit to Lake Garda.

1. Sailing - With the lake's favorable winds and gorgeous vistas, it's no wonder sailing is a popular activity here. Take a guided sailing tour or enroll in sailing classes at one of the many sailing clubs located around the lake, including Fraglia Vela Malcesine and Circolo Vela Torbole.

2. Hiking - The verdant hills around Lake Garda feature numerous well-marked hiking trails suitable for beginners and seasoned hikers alike. One of the most popular routes is the 'Old Ponale Road,' which leads from Riva del Garda to Pregasina, offering breathtaking views along the way.

3. Cycling - Biking enthusiasts can tackle the scenic bike path circling Lake Garda or venture into picturesque towns like Peschiera del Garda and Desenzano del Garda. For a more leisurely cycling outing, try the cycle path from Lazise to Bardolino or Malcesine to Torbole along the eastern shore.

4. Wildlife Parks - Nature lovers should not miss out on visiting Parco Natura Viva or Parco Giardino Sigurtà. Parco Natura Viva is a wildlife safari park housing hundreds of animals; visitors explore various ecosystems while getting up close and personal with their inhabitants. Parco Giardino Sigurtà is an expansive botanic garden rich in biodiversity, perfect for a relaxing day surrounded by flora and fauna.

5. Golf - Golf aficionados will find several courses scattered around Lake Garda appealing to different skill levels. The Arzaga Golf Club in Calvagese della Riviera features both 9-hole and 18-hole courses, while the Palazzo Arzaga Hotel, Golf & Spa Resort offers sweeping views of the lake as you enjoy its Jack Nicklaus II-designed course.

6. Adventure Parks - For adrenaline-seeking visitors, the region offers adventure parks like the Gardaland and Caneva Aquapark. Gardaland features fantastic rides and attractions for the entire family and is Italy's largest amusement park. For those who prefer water adventures, Caneva Aquapark provides exhilarating water slides and splash pools to cool down during hot summer days.

Lake Garda's beautiful landscape not only provides stunning vistas but also a playground for those who appreciatethe outdoors and a love for wine. From sailing the azure waters to hiking lush hills, visitors can participate in outdoor activities while indulging in wine tasting experiences unique to the region.

MILAN TRAVEL GUIDE 2023

Lake Maggiore

Our journey in exploring Lake Maggiore begins through the picturesque town of Stresa, enjoying the splendors of the Borromean Islands, and be in awe of the opulent Villa Taranto. Explore the fortress of Rocca di Angera, and unearth its rich history.

And beyond these fascinating towns and attractions, Lake Maggiore also boasts striking gardens and palaces that showcase centuries of art and architecture. Soar high above this earthly paradise with scenic cable car rides, offering breathtaking panoramic views you'll cherish for years to come. Let us guide you through this unforgettable odyssey as you discover the many wonders Lake Maggiore has to offer.

MILAN TRAVEL GUIDE 2023

Towns and Attractions in Lake Maggiore

Now let's explore some of the most captivating towns and attractions around Lake Maggiore, including Stresa, the Borromean Islands, Villa Taranto, and Rocca di Angera.

Stresa

Nestled on the western shore of Lake Maggiore, the charming town of Stresa is a paradise for tourists. Renowned for its scenic beauty and breathtaking views of the lake, visitors can stroll along the picturesque promenade while admiring extravagant villas and lush gardens. The town's historic center is adorned with narrow streets, bustling piazzas, vibrant cafes and shops featuring local crafts.

Stresa is also an ideal base for exploring the surrounding attractions such as the *Mottarone Cable Car* ride offering panoramic views of Lake Maggiore, or venturing to nearby parks such as *Parco della Villa Pallavicino*, which boasts botanical gardens, exotic animals and scenic trails.

Borromean Islands

Located near Stresa are the enchanting Borromean Islands - *Isola Bella, Isola Madre* and *Isola dei Pescatori*. Their beauty has captivated artists and poets for centuries. Each island has its unique charm that draws numerous visitors each year.

Isola Bella houses an opulent Baroque palace - *Palazzo Borromeo* - with terraced gardens cascading down to the water's edge. Once inside, visitors can admire grand salons adorned with priceless artworks and intricate frescoes.

Isola Madre features an elegant villa surrounded by English-style gardens filled with rare flora and fauna. This remarkable botanical sanctuary is home to free-roaming peacocks who delight visitors with their majestic plumage.

Finally, *Isola dei Pescatori*, also known as Fishermen's Island, is the only inhabited island of the three. Its narrow cobbled streets, charming houses and lively waterfront restaurants offer an authentic and relaxing experience for those seeking a taste of local culture.

Villa Taranto
On the western shore of Lake Maggiore lies the extraordinary Villa Taranto – a sprawling estate boasting 16 acres of verdant gardens. Established in the 1930s by *Scotsman Neil McEacharn*, Villa Taranto houses an impressive collection of over 20,000 plant species.

Visitors can wander through meandering paths lined with vibrant flowerbeds and ancient trees while marveling at fountains, sculptures, and ponds teeming with life. Highlights include the *Dahlia Maze, Water Lily Greenhouse*, and *Japanese Garden*. Visitors during springtime can rejoice witnessing the spectacles of thousands of tulips in bloom.

Rocca di Angera

Rocca di Angera is a medieval castle perched atop a hill on Lake Maggiore's eastern shore, overlooking the quaint town of Angera. This impressive fortress dating back to the 13th century is owned by the Borromeo family and still retains its ancient character.

A visit to this majestic castle offers not only stunning panoramic views but also a glimpse into its storied past. Guided tours lead guests through ornately decorated rooms filled with frescoes, statues, and tapestries while recounting legends surrounding this historic stronghold.

One noteworthy attraction within the castle is the *Doll and Toy Museum* showcasing an extensive collection of dolls, toys, and miniatures from different eras, providing insight into childhood during bygone times.

In conclusion, Lake Maggiore's captivating towns and attractions offer a rich tapestry of experiences that cater to diverse interests. Exploring these idyllic locations allows visitors to immerse themselves in the beauty of Italian lakes and take-home lasting memories from their enchanting sojourn.

Gardens, Palaces, and Scenic Cable Car Rides

Lake Maggiore, often overshadowed by its more famous neighbor, Lake Como, is in fact a hidden gem with lush gardens, luxurious palaces, and thrilling aerial adventures waiting to be discovered. This section takes you through the botanical wonders, royal splendors, and scenic cable car rides that grace the sweeping landscape of this striking Italian lake.

Gardens

1. Isola Madre: The largest of the Borromean Islands offers up a botanical paradise in its extensive gardens which cover nearly eight hectares. Overlooking the calm waters of the lake, Isola Madre's exotic plants are nourished by the Mediterranean climate. Visitors are delighted by rare species such as the Kashmir cypress while being entertained by wandering peacocks displaying their colorful plumage.

2. Villa Taranto: The brainchild of Scottish Captain Neil McEacharn who acquired it in 1931; Villa Taranto boasts nearly twenty acres of verdant nature. Embark on a leisurely stroll amid over 20,000 plant varieties and take in sights of charming streams dotted with fountains, fragrant flower beds, tropical greenhouses and water lily ponds.

3. Alpinia Garden: Situated above Stresa at an altitude of 800 meters, Alpinia Garden rewards all who venture here with a remarkable array of alpine flora as well as an unrivaled view of Lake Maggiore and the surrounding mountains. It is a haven for nature enthusiasts who will adore spending hours among the 1,000 plant species gracing this mountain garden.

MILAN TRAVEL GUIDE 2023

Palaces

1. Palazzo Borromeo: Dominating Isola Bella is Palazzo Borromeo; its baroque beauty standing as testament to artistry and opulence. Within its walls lie grandiose reception halls adorned with tapestries and precious frescoes, an art gallery boasting works of renowned Italian artists, and a captivating grotto displaying mythological figures. The palace provides visitors with insights into the lives of 17th-century nobility and the splendor that surrounded them.

2. Rocca d'Angera: A lakeside fortress found in the quaint village of Angera houses the enchanting Rocca d'Angera complete with its gardens, medieval courtyards, and well-preserved frescoes. Marvel at its collection of dolls and toys as you immerse yourself in the whimsical atmosphere or take in the panoramic lake views from atop its historic walls.

Scenic Cable Car Rides

1. Mottarone Cable Car: A journey via the Stresa-Alpino-Mottarone Cable Car is not to be missed when visiting Lake Maggiore. As you glide gracefully up to the summit of Mottarone, prepare to be awestruck by 360-degree views that encompass seven picturesque lakes and even a glimpse of majestic Monte Rosa. For thrill-seekers, an adrenaline-pumping descent onboard a thrilling Alpyland coaster ride offers another way to explore this panoramic realm.

2. Laveno-Mombello Cable Car: One cannot mention cable car rides in Lake Maggiore without highlighting the Laveno-Mombello bucket-lift. Those brave enough to step into its open-air cabins are rewarded with breathtaking views of Lake Maggiore and the Swiss Alps on their ascent to Sasso del Ferro. Make sure to have your camera handy for those unforgettable moments.

To fully appreciate the beauty and grandeur of these treasures during your Lake Maggiore sojourn, be sure to schedule stops at each of these attractions in your itinerary for an immersive Italian Lakes escapade.

MILAN TRAVEL GUIDE 2023

Lake Orta

Here, we'll explore the charming towns and attractions that make Lake Orta a must-visit for any traveler. Discover the enchanting streets of Orta San Giulio, walk the sacred path at Sacro Monte di Orta, and admire the architectural masterpiece that is Villa Crespi.

We will also set foot on the mystical Isola San Giulio, where local legends come to life. Throughout your journey, embrace the tranquility and spiritual retreats Lake Orta offers, making this corner of Italy an unforgettable experience.

MILAN TRAVEL GUIDE 2023

Towns and Attractions in Lake Orta

Lake Orta, often considered Italy's best-kept secret, is a magical gem tucked away in the Piedmont region. This spectacular destination captivates visitors with its stunning landscape and charming towns that hold centuries of history. Let's dicover a memorable journey through Lake Orta's enchanting towns and attractions: Orta San Giulio, Isola San Giulio, Sacro Monte di Orta, and Villa Crespi.

Orta San Giulio

Located on the eastern shore of Lake Orta is the captivating town of Orta San Giulio, a place that has maintained its medieval charm throughout centuries. Cobblestone streets and hidden courtyards are lined with pastel-colored houses adorned by flower-filled balconies. As you stroll along the lakeshore, you'll be mesmerized by the breathtaking views of the lake and surrounding hills.

The town's centerpiece is *Piazza Motta*, an enchanting square enclosed by historical buildings and palazzos. Here, you'll find inviting cafés and trattorias overlooking the sparkling lake, offering traditional Italian cuisine and local wines. Do not miss out on savoring delicate dishes such as risotto with persico (perch) sourced from the lake itself.

Other notable attractions in Orta San Giulio include the Church of *Santa Maria Assunta*. Built in the 15th century, this gothic church showcases impressive frescoes depicting scenes from the Old Testament.

After exploring the church's interior, make your way up to *Sacro Monte di Orta* for a spiritual experience like no other.

Isola San Giulio

A short boat ride from Orta San Giulio takes you to the mystical Isola San Giulio - a small island residing in the heart of Lake Orta. Legend has it that St. Julius vanquished dragons and other dangerous creatures inhabiting the island before founding a monastery in the 4th century.

Today, Isola San Giulio is home to the *Basilica di San Giulio*, built on ancient Roman ruins. The basilica is renowned for its splendid frescoes and intricately designed wooden pulpit, both dating back to the 15th century. As you step inside, the choral chanting of nuns gently echoing through the halls will transport you to days gone by.

Take a reflective walk around the island on the *"Path of Silence,"* absorbing the tranquility and serenity this haven has to offer. Along the path, be inspired by strategically placed quotes and phrases in numerous languages urging visitors to contemplate nature, love, and life.

Sacro Monte di Orta

On a hill overlooking Orta San Giulio, Sacro Monte di Orta is a UNESCO World Heritage site steeped in spiritual significance. Established in the 16th century, this sacred complex boasts twenty chapels dedicated to St. Francis of Assisi, each depicting episodes from his life through striking frescoes and terracotta statues.

A walking path winds around Sacro Monte through lush gardens, inviting visitors to reflect and meditate while exploring this exceptional place. This haven provides a harmonious blend of art, faith, and nature that captivates visitors with each visit.

Villa Crespi

Stepping into Villa Crespi is like being transported into a fairy tale setting from Arabian Nights. Built in 1879 by wealthy Italian cotton merchant *Cristoforo Benigno Crespi*, this Moorish-style villa is now a luxurious hotel and renowned restaurant serving Lake Orta's visitors.

The richly decorated interiors exude opulence stemming from Islamic art influences – intricately carved wooden doors, ornate plasterwork, and stunning mosaic tiles adorn every corner of this architectural gem.

Besides offering lavish accommodations with unparalleled lake views, Villa Crespi features a gourmand's paradise - the two-Michelin-starred restaurant led by celebrated chef Antonino Cannavacciuolo. This fine dining experience offers an unforgettable blend of Italian tradition and contemporary culinary techniques, ensuring that every dish is a symphony of flavors.

As you wander through Lake Orta's picturesque towns and attractions, allow its captivating allure to transport you to a world of breathtaking beauty and serenity. From the medieval town of Orta San Giulio to the divine pathways of Isola San Giulio, and from Sacro Monte di Orta's chapels to lavish Villa Crespi – each destination offersa unique and unforgettable experience for every traveler.

Whether seeking tranquility, spiritual reflection, or indulging in the rich tradition of Italian cuisine, Lake Orta's enchanting towns and attractions offer an oasis of magic and adventure. Every corner of the lake holds stories and moments ready to be discovered, making it a destination that warrants several visits.

Tranquility, Spiritual Retreats, and Local Legends

Lake Orta, a jewel in the crown of Northern Italy's lake district, is known for its serene charm and unspoiled beauty. This enchanting body of water has long been a haven for those seeking tranquility and spiritual nourishment. Its picturesque landscapes have inspired countless artists and legends over the centuries.

Tranquility

Nestled among rolling hills and verdant forests, Lake Orta exudes an air of peacefulness that captivates both locals and visitors alike. A world away from the bustling cities and tourist hubs that have come to define Italy, the lake offers a serene escape from everyday life.

Historically, nobles frequented Lake Orta as their preferred getaway – a place where they could revel in its calming atmosphere. Today, tourists are drawn to the lake's tranquil shores, where they can enjoy leisurely strolls along waterfront promenades or unwind beside its shimmering waters.

One particularly charming spot-on Lake Orta is the lakeside town of Orta San Giulio. With its narrow-cobbled streets and traditional architecture, this medieval town has retained much of its authentic character. Visitors can wander through its winding streets, relax at a lakeside café, or contemplate life while gazing across the water at the lush island of San Giulio.

Spiritual Retreats

Lake Orta's mystical allure has drawn spiritual seekers for centuries. The island of San Giulio, located at the heart of the lake, is home to an ancient basilica and a Benedictine monastery. As legend has it, Saint Giulio himself founded the basilica in the 4th century after subduing monsters that had terrorized locals for generations.

Over time, various religious orders have inhabited the island; today, it is home to a community of cloistered nuns who continue the centuries-old tradition of prayer and contemplation. Visitors to San Giulio can access the island by boat and immerse themselves in its spiritual atmosphere, walking the Way of Silence and Meditation – a peaceful circuit enveloping the island.

On the mainland, the Sacro Monte di Orta is another significant spiritual site. Set high above Orta San Giulio, this UNESCO World Heritage Site features 20 chapels adorned with frescoes and statues that pay homage to Saint Francis of Assisi. Dotted among ancient woods, these sacred spaces provide an inspirational retreat for those seeking spiritual growth and renewal.

Local Legends

The beauty of Lake Orta has inspired many legends and stories, which have been passed down through generations. One such tale is that of a giant serpent that lives beneath the lake's surface. Known as *Cusius*, this legendary creature is said to protect the lake's pristine waters and has been spotted by locals throughout history.

A more recent myth stems from *Villa Crespi*, a stunning 19th-century palace erected by an Italian cotton baron named Cristoforo Crespi. According to legend, Lord Byron wrote his famous poem *"Childe Harold's Pilgrimage"* while staying at Villa Crespi – although there is no concrete evidence to support this story.

In addition to these legends, Lake Orta abounds with intriguing tales of secret passageways, hidden treasures, and more. Visitors may stumble upon captivating lore during their stay or even uncover new stories to add to the area's rich tapestry of myths.

MILAN TRAVEL GUIDE 2023

Lake Orta remains one of Italy's most alluring destinations for those seeking tranquility, spiritual growth, and fascinating legends. With its idyllic landscapes and enchanting atmosphere, the lake offers a unique and unforgettable experience for travelers looking to escape from life's rapid pace.

As you journey onward in your travels, consider delving more deeply into the wonder that is Lake Orta. Immerse yourself in its stillness, walk the sacred paths and chapels, and listen closely to the whispers of its age-old legends. In doing so, you may find yourself profoundly transformed by the beauty and mystique that make this Italian gem so captivating.

MILAN TRAVEL GUIDE 2023

Insider Tips for the Italian Lakes

Our insider's perspective will take you on a journey to experience the enchanting beauty of Italy's lake region like never before. Discover the best viewpoints and scenic spots to capture breathtaking panoramas, immerse yourself in authentic local culture by attending vibrant festivals and events, and unleash your inner adventurer with recommendations for exhilarating hikes, serene boat trips, and invigorating cycling routes. Embark on an unforgettable adventure with this indispensable guide!

Best Viewpoints and Scenic Spots

1. Villa Balbianello, Lake Como: Perched atop a wooded promontory, Villa Balbianello offers panoramic views of Lake Como. Stroll through its terraced gardens adorned with azaleas, rhododendrons, and ancient cypress trees or book a guided tour to explore its elegant interiors replete with priceless art.

2. Monte Mottarone, Lake Maggiore: A short cable car ride from Stresa takes you up to Monte Mottarone, where you can enjoy breathtaking views of Lake Maggiore and surrounding Alpine peaks. The 360-degree panorama showcases seven lakes (Maggiore,

Orta, Mergozzo, Varese, Comabbio, Monate and Biandronno) and a myriad of picturesque towns below.

3. Rocca Borromeo di Angera, Lake Maggiore: An imposing fortress on a tall hill near Angera town overlooks Lake Maggiore and offers splendid views. Explore its historic chambers displaying frescoes, weaponry, and armor; then visit the Doll & Toy Museum housed within the castle walls.

4. Bella Island viewpoint (on Isola Bella), Lake Maggiore: Board a boat from Stresa and cross over to Isola Bella at Lake Maggiore's center for awe-inspiring scenery of the lake, its shoreline, and scattered islands. Saunter through the terraced gardens of the Borromeo Palace and take in the charming tableau.

5. Punta San Vigilio, Lake Garda: A narrow peninsula jutting into the turquoise waters of Lake Garda hides the cozy hamlet of Punta San Vigilio. Wander the tranquil lanes past beautiful villas, a picturesque harbor, and make your way to a scenic lookout for majestic vistas of the largest Italian lake.

Local Festivals and Events

1. Limone sul Garda Lemon Festival: A cherished tradition in Limone sul Garda village on Lake Garda, citizens demonstrate their reverence for lemon cultivation through an annual summer festival. Delight in live music, food stalls offering lemon-infused delicacies, and artisan crafts at this refreshing event.

2. Cantine Aperte: Wineries around Lake Garda and Franciacorta in Lombardy fling open their doors for a weekend each May during the "Cantine Aperte" celebration. Wine enthusiasts can taste delightful local wines from participating estates while enjoying guided tours and picturesque scenery.

3. Luci d'Artista (Artist's Lights), Salò, Lake Garda: Every December, Salò's historic center is transformed into a mesmerizing wonderland of light installations crafted by local artists. The unique blend of tradition and contemporary artistry makes it an unforgettable experience.

4. Stresa Music Festival: Immerse yourself in classical tunes at this annual June-July cultural extravaganza on Lake Maggiore's shores. Nurtured in sublime surroundings, passionate performances by renowned artists at prestigious venues like Villa Pallavicino or Isola Bella will leave you spellbound.

Recommendations For Hiking, Boating, And Cycling

The Italian Lakes, a captivating region in Northern Italy, boasts a landscape that promises a myriad of outdoor activities for adventure seekers and nature lovers. Here, we will delve into the best insider tips for exploring the charming Italian Lakes through hiking, boating, and cycling adventures.

Recommendations for Hiking

1. Lake Como's Greenway Trail: A picturesque 10km path along the western shore of Lake Como, this well-marked trail connects Colonno to Cadenabbia di Griante. Follow the signposts with a green, white, and red stripe as you pass through quaint villages, terraced landscapes, and ancient ruins. Both accessible and moderately challenging, this trail suits hikers of all levels.

2. Monte Isola on Lake Iseo: For a more immersive experience steeped in history and local culture, visit Monte Isola - the largest lake island in Europe. Accessible via a short ferry ride from Sulzano or Sale Marasino, numerous routes wind through olive groves and charming hamlets offering spectacular views over Lake Iseo.

3. Val Grande National Park near Lake Maggiore: A veritable paradise for experienced hikers seeking solitude in unspoiled wilderness areas. The park's rugged terrain features ancient mule tracks and numerous trekking routes of varying lengths. Discover hidden valleys and breathtaking panoramas as you conquer the park's heights.

Recommendations for Boating

1. Hire a private boat on Lake Como: Offering unmatched freedom to explore the lake's picturesque shoreline at your leisure, renting a boat (with or without a skipper) becomes an unforgettable experience. Visit popular towns like Bellagio or secluded access-only shores perfect for swimming and picnicking.

2. Public ferry cruise on Lake Maggiore: Experience the grandeur of Lake Maggiore on board one of its public ferries connecting Stresa, Baveno, Pallanza, and the Borromean Islands. In addition to ease of transportation, this trip offers stunning views of the villas and gardens lining the shores.

3. Brissago Islands tour on Lake Lugano: Embark on a guided boat tour departing from Lugano and visit Canton Ticino's natural gem - the Brissago Islands. Marvel at the botanical garden boasting thousands of exotic plant species and submerge yourself in a Mediterranean atmosphere right in the Swiss Alps.

Recommendations for Cycling

1. Mincio River cycle path: This well-maintained 45km route connecting Peschiera del Garda on Lake Garda to Mantua offers a flat, family-friendly excursion through picturesque countryside. Pedal alongside the river as you pass quaint villages and historic sites such as Sigurtà Park and Valeggio sul Mincio.

2. Lake Varese circular route: A 28km loop mixing lakeside scenery with glimpses of pre-Alpine peaks. Suitable for cyclists with moderate fitness levels, this mostly paved route passes by numerous waterfront towns such as Gavirate, Schiranna Natural Park, and Cazzago Brabbia's marshes.

3. Brescia's Franciacorta wine region: For an unforgettable cycling adventure combining vineyards, history, and delicious cuisine, head to Franciacorta. Choose from several itineraries between Lake Iseo and Brescia, pedaling through rolling hills dotted with medieval villages and enjoying stops at family-owned wineries along the way.

With these insider tips revealing hidden gems and exclusive experiences, your Italian Lakes adventure will transcend ordinary sightseeing – expect to uncover nature's breathtaking beauty while basking in vibrant local culture that infuses the region's spirit.

MILAN TRAVEL GUIDE 2023

Smart Tips for Budget Travelers

This last chapter will ensure you make the most out of your journey without breaking the bank. Unearth hidden gems and adopt savvy strategies to maximize your experience in Milan and its breathtaking surroundings. We'll explore affordable accommodation options, guaranteeing comfort without compromising quality.

Additionally, we'll navigate through budget-friendly dining choices and transportation methods, allowing you to indulge in the local delicacies and venture the captivating sights. Embark on an unforgettable adventure while staying economically wise.

Affordable Accommodation Options

Finding affordable accommodation in Milan is essential for budget travelers. Hostels, B&Bs, and budget hotels are some of the best options for lower costs while still enjoying comfort and convenience.

1. Hostels: Milan has plenty of hostels catering to different needs and preferences. The city center-based hostels tend to cost slightly more but offer excellent proximity to attractions. Consider New Generation Hostel or Ostello Bello if location is your priority.

2. Bed & Breakfasts: B&Bs provide an intimate atmosphere akin to being a guest in someone's home. They often include breakfast, which can save you money on meals. Some popular options are La Casa di Leonardo and B&B Hotel Milano Cenisio Garibaldi.

3. Airbnb: Airbnb offers a diverse range of properties, from private rooms to entire apartments or homes. This platform allows travelers to tailor their accommodation based on their specific needs and budget constraints. Look for properties located slightly outside the city center for the best deals.

4. Budget Hotels: Another feasible alternative for budget travelers is opting for a more affordable hotel. While they may not have all the amenities of a luxury hotel, several options provide clean and comfortable rooms at reasonable rates. Booking in advance or during off-peak periods will increase your chances of finding a bargain. Try Ibis Milano Centro or MEININGER Milano Garibaldi, known for their affordability and great locations.

Budget-Friendly Dining and Transportation

Experiencing Milan's culinary scene does not require spending excessive amounts on luxury dining experiences. You can still savor delicious Italian cuisine at local eateries or street food vendors without stretching your wallet.

MILAN TRAVEL GUIDE 2023

1. Affordable Eats: Although Milan boasts gourmet restaurants, it is also home to many pizzerias, trattorias, and paninotecas that serve reasonably-priced meals. Highlights include Luini Panzerotti (renowned for its mouthwatering panzerotti) and Pizzeria Da Zero.

2. Grocery Shopping: For even more savings, consider buying groceries and preparing meals at your accommodation. Many hostels and B&Bs offer kitchenettes for guest use. Milan's local markets, such as Navigli Market and Mercato V Alpini, boast fresh produce, deli items, and cheeses for budget-friendly meal planning.

3. Aperitivo: When in Milan, don't miss out on the "aperitivo" culture. This pre-dinner ritual offers an opportunity to sample various snacks served with a drink at a reasonable price during the early evening. Check out Ceresio 7 or Mag Bar for an inexpensive yet satisfying aperitivo experience.

Saving money on transportation is another crucial aspect of budget travel in Milan. Instead of using taxis or ride-sharing services, take advantage of public transport options.

1. Public Transportation: Milan's public transportation network comprises buses, trams, and a metro system. Purchase daily or multi-day passes available at any *ATM (Azienda Trasporti Milanesi)* ticket office or vending machine to save costs on multiple rides.

2. Bike-sharing: Rent bikes to explore the city while getting exercise. BikeMi offers affordable day passes allowing you to explore Milan's attractions and beautiful parks on two wheels.

3. Walking Tours: Join free walking tours conducted by local guides who share their knowledge of Milan's history and culture. It's an excellent way to discover hidden gems without spending money on guided tours.

By following these smart tips for budget travelers, you can fully enjoy the charm of Milan and the Italian Lakes without compromising your wallet. After all, extraordinary memories are priceless regardless of how much you spend. Happy travels!

CONCLUSION

As we conclude our journey through **"Milan Travel Guide 2023,"** there is no doubt that the unique charm, history, and natural beauty of this region have left an indelible impression on our hearts. Strolling through Milan's captivating streets, we've explored its rich historical background, marveled at iconic landmarks such as the *Duomo di Milano* and *Sforza Castle*, and tasted its diverse culinary delights. We've immersed ourselves in Milan's thriving art and design scene, experiencing the masterpieces of *Brera Art Gallery* and the cutting-edge collections of the *Museum of the Twentieth Century*.

Venturing beyond city limits, we've encountered enchanting towns nestled amongst towering mountains and embraced the tranquility of Italian Lakes, each with its distinctive allure. From Lake Como's picturesque villages of *Bellagio* and *Varenna* to Lake Garda's bustling resorts and wine-tasting opportunities; from the regal majesty of Lake Maggiore's *Borromean Islands* to the spiritual mystique of Lake Orta – our spirits have been elevated by experiences that transcended ordinary expectations.

The insider tips offered throughout the guide have unlocked hidden treasures and lesser-known attractions which we might have otherwise overlooked. Our memories are filled not only with Milan's must-sees but also with countless gems that only locals know about. Whether joining the locals in vibrant neighborhoods or partaking in wine tastings, we've delved into Italian culture and savored authentic moments.

We've also embraced smart budget travel techniques, making cherished memories without breaking the bank. Our guide shared affordable accommodation options alongside budget-friendly dining experiences, enabling us to stretch our travel dollars further while ensuring comfort levels remained high.

In conclusion, this comprehensive guide has been an invaluable companion on a life-changing journey through Milan and the Italian Lakes region. As we fondly reflect upon our adventures, may they inspire both seasoned travelers and first-time explorers alike to immerse themselves in all the wonders that Italy has to offer. "Milan Travel Guide 2023" has truly unlocked a world of unforgettable experiences, vividly etching Milan and its enchanting surroundings into our hearts, forever enriching our lives.

Final Tips and Recommendations for A Perfect Trip

As you wrap up your journey through Milan and the Italian Lakes, let's offer some final advice to ensure that your trip is seamless and enjoyable.

MILAN TRAVEL GUIDE 2023

1. Plan your itinerary in advance: Although it's always nice to be spontaneous, having a well-planned itinerary can save you time and stress. Research the attractions, museums, and sights that interest you most, prioritize them, and then allocate specific times for visiting them.

2. Learn some essential phrases in Italian: Even though English is widely spoken in Milan and around the Italian Lakes, knowing a few basic phrases can go a long way with locals. Saying *"please," "thank you,"* and *"excuse me"* in Italian can make your trip more authentic and amicable.

3. Pack for the season: Milan's weather can vary greatly depending on the time of year. Be prepared for hot summers and cold winters by packing appropriate clothing.

4. Utilize public transportation: Milan has an excellent public transportation system that includes buses, trams, and the metro. Familiarize yourself with the city's transport options to reach all corners of this bustling metropolis.

5. Enjoy local cuisine: Beyond just pizza and pasta, the culinary scene in Milan offers a vast array of gastronomic delights like risotto alla Milanese or osso buco. Don't forget to taste regional dishes while exploring the towns around the Italian Lakes as well.

Encouragement To Explore Other Regions of Italy

MILAN TRAVEL GUIDE 2023

Milan and its surrounding lakes are just the beginning of what Italy has to offer travelers. Make sure to venture beyond these destinations as you continue to explore the beauty and history of this exquisite country.

1. Head north towards Lake Garda or Lake Como for an adventure-filled day amidst idyllic scenery perfect for hiking, sailing, or simply relaxing by the water.

2. Discover other captivating cities like Florence, Rome, and Venice, each with its unique charm, architecture, and culture waiting to be experienced.

3. Unearth the lesser-known yet enchanting regions of Italy, from the rugged coastlines of Liguria to the picturesque countryside of Tuscany.

4. Immerse yourself in Italy's traditional festivals and events, which showcase vibrant local customs and delicious dishes across various regions. Popular celebrations include Carnevale di Venezia in Venice or Palio di Siena in Tuscany.

5. Develop a new appreciation for Italian wine by visiting vineyards across diverse regions, such as Chianti in Tuscany or Valpolicella in Veneto. Gain insight into their winemaking processes while sampling some of the world's finest wines straight from the source.

By applying these tips and recommendations to your journey, you can create unforgettable memories. However, don't stop at Milan – take every opportunity to explore the rest of Italy's captivating regions as each holds unique surprises that promise to make your experience even more memorable.

As we come to the end of this comprehensive exploration through "Milan Travel Guide 2023: The Complete Guide to Discover Milan and The Italian Lakes," it is only fitting that we take a moment to reflect on the rich tapestry of history, culture, and natural beauty that we've encountered along the way.

The city of Milan itself stands as a testament to the long and varied history of Italy, its opulent architecture and cobbled streets telling tales that span from ancient Roman times to the modern era. As we navigated these intricate urban landscapes, we were reminded of the deep roots from which Milan has sprung, anchoring its place as an icon of European civilization.

Closing Thoughts on The Tapestry of History, Culture, And Natural Beauty

Throughout our journey, we have been privy to the dazzling array of art and culture that flourishes within the city's nexus. From its world-famous museums such as *Pinacoteca di Brera* to the breathtaking sight of *The Last Supper by Leonardo da Vinci*, each piece contributed a vibrant stitch in the fabric of Milano's cultural identity.

MILAN TRAVEL GUIDE 2023

But Milan is not just a bustling city – it also serves as a gateway to exploring the Italian Lakes' ethereal beauty. We broke free from urban confines and ventured into nature's embrace at Lake Como, Lake Garda, Lake Maggiore, and Lake Orta. It was here among pristine waters, charming lakeside villas, and verdant mountainside gardens that we reveled in Italy's majestic natural splendor.

In conclusion, our exploration has brought us face to face with moments that interweave strands from the past with threads of the present. Every corner unveiled new aspects within this tapestry – where vibrant passions for food, fashion, music, and more come together in synchrony. Italy has left us enraptured by its warmth charm and elegance throughout our explorations in Milan and nearby lakes.

Through these closing thoughts, we hope that your own journey into Milan and the Italian Lakes will be imbued with a newfound appreciation for this vibrant tapestry of history, culture, and natural beauty. Delve into this panorama of experiences, leave no thread unexamined and immerse yourself in all that Milan has to offer – an enchanting adventure awaits.

All the best,

Jimmy Vitale

Printed in Great Britain
by Amazon